FISCALITÉ EN EUROPE

CONFÉDÉRATION FISCALE EUROPÉENNE
(C.F.E.)

Fiscalité en Europe

PREMIER CONGRÈS EUROPÉEN DES CONSEILS FISCAUX
ERSTER EUROPA-KONGRESS DER STEUERBERATER
FIRST EUROPEAN TAX CONSULTANTS CONGRESS

STRASBOURG

1978

SPRINGER-SCIENCE+BUSINESS MEDIA, B.V.

CONFÉDÉRATION FISCALE EUROPÉENNE

Siège Social: 9, rue Richepanse, F-75008 Paris

Secrétariat Général: Dechenstrasse 14 (Postfach 1340), D-5300 Bonn 1, Tél. (0 22 21) 63.85.58, Télex 8 869 487

ISBN 978-90-200-0578-3 ISBN 978-94-017-1482-2 (eBook)
DOI 10.1007/978-94-017-1482-2

Originally published by Kluwer Law and Taxation, The Netherlands in 1979

Published on behalf of the Confédération Fiscale Européenne.

First European Tax Consultants' Congress

13th / 14th October 1978 in Strasbourg

Theme: Fiscalité en Europe

The Confédération Fiscale Européenne (C.F.E.) is the association of professional organizations of tax consultants from the countries of the European Communities. Its function is to represent the professional interests of tax consultants from the countries of the European Communities, in particular to foster relations with the Authorities of national and international organs, to pave the way for the standardization of national professional legislations and to influence the shaping of directives on establishment and services in the tax consulting field. It is anxious to keep the Authorities of the Communities informed of the experiences made by all those practising the profession in the various fields of taxation, and in particular it wishes to participate in the activities concerning the progressive standardization of the national tax legislations.

There exists already a network of relations in many spheres of private enterprise within the member states of the European Communities which affects the taxation of entreprise. Tax experts are not consulted exclusively on matters of taxation by their business clients, but are also consulted on matters of economics, business administration and commercial law. Consequently, comprehensive information on present-day events of taxation in each of the member states of the European Communities has become a fundamental condition for tax consulting, if it is to be effective and to take account of the European context. The meeting of tax consultants from all the states of the European Communities also contributes to the understanding of professional and economic problems as well as of those of economic policy. The First European Tax Consultants' Congress should therefore be a starting point for further meetings of tax consultants from the European countries with the purpose of exchanging views as thoroughly as possible on all aspects of the profession and on all points dealing with its practice.

Prof Dr. Albert Tiberghien
President

Contents

Opening of the Congress by the President of the C.F.E.

Professor Dr. Albert Tiberghien
Conseil Fiscal, Brussels

Translated from French by Roselle Prill du Pradal

Commissioner Burke,
Presidents,
Director Generals,
Secretary-Generals
and Directors
of the European and national organisations and institutions,
my dear colleagues,
Ladies and Gentlemen,

I wish to welcome all those who have come to the European City of Strasbourg in order to attend the First European Tax Consultants' Congress.

The Confédération Fiscale Européenne, which will celebrate its 20th anniversary in a few months is, of course, pleased that 500 tax consultants from all the countries of the European Communities as well as the presidents of their professional organisations have responded to its invitation and that even a number of other countries belonging to Europe and America are represented here. It particularly appreciates that the present Congress has given rise to great interest on the part of the European Institutions.

For this reason may I extend my welcome in particular to the representatives of the "official Europe". I regret not to be able to welcome individually all the personalities present here to-day, indeed I must refer to the list of participants where their names are included. But it is my duty to welcome in particular some high-ranking personalities who by their very presence, give our first European Congress a very high standard.

M. Pierre Pflimlin, Mayor of Strasbourg, and European of the first hour, who had accepted to speak this morning, can unfortunately not be present, as he has to be in Paris this morning. Nonetheless, may I thank him for his help in choosing Strasbourg for the Congress. I greet the persons in charge of the municipality of Strasbourg, of its University and of its "Palais des Congrès".

The European Parliament, which has its seat at Strasbourg, is represented here by the President of its
by the President of its Legal Affairs Committee
Sir Derek Walker-Smith, M. P., Q. C.,
who will speak to us this morning,
by the Secretary-General of the European Parliament
M. Hans R. Nord,
and by the Director General of the Cabinet of the President
M. Pasetti-Bombardella.

The Commission of the European Communities is here represented
by the Commissioner responsible for all taxation problems,
M. Richard Burke,
whom I wish to greet and thank especially, since he shall speak to us this morning on his views concerning tax harmonisation in Europe. He is accompanied by a number of high-ranking officers from the Commission of whom I wish to name in particular
M. Ole Bus Hendriksen,

Director-General of the Commission, whose functions also include fiscal problems.

The Council of the European Communities is represented by its Director,

M. Wolfgang Pini,

who is in charge of fiscal harmonization.

I am also happy to welcome the permanent fiscal representatives of Denmark, Ireland and the Netherlands.

The Economic and Social Committee of the European Communities has sent as its official representative its member

M. Hermann Fredersdorf,

whose function as President of the European Union of the Fiscal Officers is a token of his closeness to our profession.

Finally, the Council of Europe, whose seat is also Strasbourg and whose flag is shown in front of this Congress Centre, and whose emblem is on your brooch pins, is represented, among others, by

M. Georges Moulin,

chief of the Economic Affairs Division of the Council of Europe.

Not only do we have representatives of the European Institutions, but the States of the Community are also well represented here by a number of the highest dignitaries of the Finance, Revenue and Justice Departments.

Thus I am happy to be able to announce the Belgian Minister for Finance,

M. Gaston Geens,

who is to arrive at noon with a member of his cabinet and the Director General in charge of taxation matters, and who will deliver a speech.

We are also awaiting the arrival of the Italian Minister for Finance,

M. Franco Malfatti.

The Minister for Justice of the Federal Republic of Germany is represented by

M. Martin Rudolph, Ministerialdirector.

We are also honoured by the presence of

Dr. Gerd Pfeiffer,

President of the Bundesgerichtshof, the Supreme Court for civil and criminal law matters,

Prof. Dr. Heinrich List,

President of the Bundesfinanzhof, the Supreme Court for taxation questions, and

Dr. Andrea Niro,

magistrate at the Italian Supreme Court of Appeals and President of the National Association of Fiscal Judges of Italy.

In my welcoming address I could certainly not forget the UEC, the "Union Européenne des Experts Comptables, Financiers et Economiques", represented here by

M. Jacques Favier,

as well as the International Chamber of Commerce and the IFA, the International Fiscal Association, represented among others by

Dr. Heining.

Finally, may I extend a warm welcome to all our eminent and courageaous speakers,

Prof. Dr. Horst Vogel, Germany

Prof. Dr. Hendrik Hofstra, Netherlands,

Mr. Desmond Airey, United Kingdom, and

Prof. Dr. Jos Jan Couturier, Belgium.

And now, last but not least, it is you all, my dear colleagues, whom I wish to congratulate for having answered our call, and in so doing for proving that you are aware that our profession is an international one and that it is our duty to contribute to the bringing about of a Europe in which economic movement will be made easier as a result of a harmonious taxation system which does not act as a hindrance to liberties.

Ladies and Gentlemen, dear Colleagues,

In the name of the Confédération Fiscale Européenne, I declare open the First European Tax Consultants' Congress.

Tax Consultants! Who are we to attract the attention of the highest personalities from the Community, and from the world of politics, the judiciary and the administrative sector? It is not because we play an important part in economic life in helping the tax payer with his heavy tax burden? Indeed, the fiscal and para-fiscal burden which is economically of the same kind as the taxes themselves, has become very large. In 1976, all the tax payers of the nine Member States, taken together, were paying in fiscal and parafiscal levies to the State and other authorities the astonishing total amount of 1.215 billions of DM[1).]

This total is equivalent to an average 38.7 % of GNP.

In certain cases the tax amounts to 70 % or more of personal income, and much more for the highest part of the scala;

---

1) This figure is obtained by converting the national currencies at the medium rate given by the Brussels stock exchange on September 28th, 1978. The details are as follows:

Germany	432.400
France	286.151
Italy	114.954
Netherlands	100.648
Belgium	65.952
Luxembourg	2.602
United Kingdom	169.909
Ireland	6.283
Denmark	36.385
	1.215.284 million DM

it usually corresponds to 50 % of the company's profit, to which income tax must be added when dividends are payed out; inheritances are taxed at the maximum rate of 80 % or more; turnover is taxed at about 15 % sometimes 30 % and certain consumption rights correspond to 90 % of the price payed by the consumer.

It is obvious that such enormous amounts could not be levied without creating serious conflicts if revenue departments were not composed of intelligent, competent officials with a high moral standing.

But tax officials are first and foremost the servants of the State, and it is thus natural that they should place the interest of the State above that of the tax-payer even if they want to remain within the boundaries of legality and make it their daily task to understand the tax-payers' problems.

Thus the tax-payer needs a specialist who will first of all give him the necessary advice so that in making his decisions, the tax-payer can avoid unnecessary expenses or that he can at least make his decision in full knowledge of the tax burden leading from his decisions. Furthermore, this specialist must help the tax-payer in his relations with the revenue departments so as to give them information about the real situation of his client and to avoid making errors of procedure. Finally, this specialist must defend the tax-payer in his dealings with revenue departments, and if need be, in the law courts so that those upon whom it is incumbent to make a decision, may do so having heard an equally competent defence from both sides.

This specialist is above all the tax consultant. I say "above all" because, of course, I do not ignore the fact that other professionals give counsel assistance and also defend the tax-payer. I know it and I approve of it. It is not at all the intention of the tax consultant to want to monopolise the counselling, assistance and defence in fiscal matters: the tax-payer must have the right to turn to his lawyer or to his accountant, who are just as entitled to advise him as is his tax consultant. We do not either wish to suggest that the lawyer, notary or accountant cannot be tax consultants: the mere fact that the Administrative Board of the Confédération Fiscale Européenne counts lawyers and accountants among its members proves the contrary. It was in fact a lawyer, Count Lecce, who is a member of our Administrative Board, who was the first to suggest the Congress we are holding to-day, and two of our speakers have both titles: Prof. Vogel, who is tax consultant and lawyer, and Prof. Couturier, who is tax consultant and accountant.

But the tax consultant, may he have at the same time no other title or may he be at the same time lawyer or accountant, is nonetheless a specialist in taxation matters, who necessarily spends a great part of his time, and makes it known that he will put his speciality to work, to the benefit of his clients.

The tax consultant can be specialized in the taxation system of one country, or in a branch of this tax system, limiting himself for example to indirect taxes, or in the taxation of international movements etc. But, whatever his individual speciality happens to be, he will only have a right to the title of tax consultant if he spends a considerable part of his time working in the field of his speciality, which because of its complexity and its rapid evolution requires extensive experience and daily studies.

The lawyer who is a "general practitioner" is thus not a tax consultant, nor is the "pure" accountant: they only become one if they acquire special knowledge in taxation by means of experience and study, as well as on the grounds of their basic professional education.

Indeed, the tax consultant must have been educated at university level, which would entail at the same time the study of law, economics and accountancy. Legal science, because taxes are the effect of laws and are put into force according to legal regulations; economics and accountancy, because the most important taxes are applied to economic facts which are registered in documents and books of accountancy.

Since the Treaties of ECSC, Euratom, and in particular since the Treaty of Rome in 1957, taxes have acquired a European dimension which I am sure it is not necessary to demonstrate before a gathering so competent in these matters.

Tax consultants immediately understood the "revolutionary" character of the Treaty of Rome and the vital influence it was going to have on economic life and indeed on life in general. Thus the representatives of the national federations met as soon as 1958 in answer to an invitation of their French colleagues, and it is in this way that the Confédération Fiscale Européenne was founded in 1959. Its seat is in Paris and its legal background is that of an international association governed by the French Law of July 1st, 1901.

It is furthermore the occasion of the 50th anniversary of one of our members, the Institut Français des Conseils Fiscaux, whose celebrations will take place tomorrow afternoon in Strasbourg, that led us to choose the year 1978 for our first Congress.

At the moment, the Confédération Fiscale Européenne includes the national associations of Germany, Belgium, France, Ireland, Italy, the Netherlands and the United Kingdom. These associations taken together all add up to approx. 50.000 members. In Denmark and in the Grand Duchy, the title of tax consultant is not used and specialists in tax law are not united in an association. But we are pleased to have positive contacts with the organisations of accountants of these two countries, who are moreover represented at this Congress.

The Confédération Fiscale Européenne should not be confused with the "International Fiscal Association" of which many tax consultants are members, who are at the same time members of our Confédération. The I. F. A. is an important association which draws its members from all over the world, but which limits itself to the study of fiscal (tax) principles and problems, without defending the professional interests of its members who furthermore are not all tax consultants, but may be also department officials, full-time professors and enterprises. The Confédération Fiscale Européenne is, on the contrary, a professional association whose aim it is to defend the professional interests of its members.

This is why the following are the main objectives of the Confédération at the moment:

1 - to enhance professional and personal contacts among colleagues of different countries
2 - to establish bases for collaboration among the representatives of the profession of tax consultants and the representatives of the profession of lawyers and accountants
3 - to study tax problems from the point of view of adapting national legislations to the ideal of the signitaries of the Treaty of Rome
4 - to obtain from the European Communities the realization of the right of establishment and of the right to render services
5 - to obtain from the States of the EEC that the regulations governing the profession of the tax consultant be established and/or harmonized.

The present Congress places itself in the framework of the three first objectives which I have just mentioned: contacts among colleagues and among professionals from the neighbouring professions as well as the study of fiscal problems on the European scale.

But I would like to say a few words about the last two objectives: the liberalization and harmonization of the profession. The Confédération would fail in its aim if the countries of Western Europe continued to live between the narrow walls of their economies and of their national taxation: the points of contact on an international level among the different tax systems and their professionals would be far to scarce to justify the existence of a real Confédération. A simple club would suffice for the few practioners of international fiscal law ...

But things do not happen in this way in the Europe which is developing as a unity. The tax consultants know well how much everything is "internationalized" in this Europe and to what extent the tax rules of each of the Member States are abolished, amended or imposed by the Community treaties, directives or regulations, and they know that their clients are increasingly concerned by the tax laws of twp or more countries. So it was that the Confédération was founded so as to facilitate the internationalization of taxation within the Common Market and of the profession of the tax consultant.

So as to attain this aim it must be possible for the tax consultant residing in country A to enjoy the liberty of rendering services in country B, and even to establish himself in country B. The Commission of the European Communities is endeavouring for a number of years to prepare the directives necessary for the liberalization of the rendering of services and the right of establishment. Many stumbling stones have hampered the putting into words of directives answering the hopes of all those concerned.

Nevertheless, I feel that the greatest hindrance in this regard is the fact that tax consultants, and for that matter also the accountants, are not governed in all the different countries by comparable national legislations. The setting up of directives concerning the medical and legal professions was the fruit of years of work, but they have finally been put into force, whereas the texts which are in the process of preparation regarding tax consultants and accountants have scarcely progressed and I am afraid that we may have to wait a long time yet before our directives come into force. On the other hand the directive "lawyers" has been the cause of temporary new distortions since the lawyers have obtained the liberalisation of their work in the fiscal field while this is still not the case for tax consultants and accountants.

Why then have the doctor and the lawyer already obtained satisfaction? Is it not because they are subjected to comparable laws in the different countries?

This is the main reason why the Confédération Fiscale Européenne has expressed the hope that the profession of tax consultants be legally organized in each country and that this legal organization be harmonious, i. e. comparable.

How far have we got in this field in the nine countries?

In Germany tax consultants are subjected to a legal system comparable to that of the lawyer. This legislation started in 1935 with the "Rechtsberatungsmißbrauchsgesetz" in 1937, the title of "Steuerberater" became protected; in 1943 a chamber of tax consultants was founded ("Kammer der Steuerberater"); but the present legislation is that of the "Steuerberatungsgesetz" (tax consulting law), which determines the law of the profession in general. There exists in that country a real order of tax consultants, to which only those can have success who have had a specific university education followed by four years practical experience and a final examination at the end of that period; and they are subjected to strict professional discipline. The profession is open to lawyers and accountants who, in this way, can belong to more than one order. The monopoly of tax law is shared among tax consultants, lawyers and accountants.

In France, the law of 31 December 1971 has established the protected title of "conseil juridique" (legal counsel), but the legal counsel specialized in fiscal matters is endowed with the title of "conseil juridique et fiscal" (legal and fiscal counsel) which is also protected.

In Italy, the title of tax consultant does not exist as such, but tax consultants are collectively called "tributaristi"; they are lawyers, "ragioneri" (accountants) and "dottori commercialisti". Their (collective) title of "tributarista" is not protected, and they do not hold the monopoly to defend the tax payers before the administrative courts.

In none of the other countries are tax consultants subjected to a special legislation; they are even seldom mentioned - e. g. in Belgium, they are subjected to special sanctions - but nowhere is their title protected, or are they given a monopoly whatsoever, or do they have to have had a special professional training or discipline. It is thus little surprising that there should be in these countries besides tax consultants of a high professional and moral standing, professionals who are lacking in one of these two essential qualities.

One of the objectives of the founders of the Confédération Fiscale Européenne was precisely to unite the national groups of tax consultants which demand from their members a professional training at university level and a moral, civil and fraternal conduct above all criticism.

Ladies and Gentlemen, my dear Colleagues,

During this Congress you will hear Mr. Burke, Commissioner of the European Communities, who is also in charge of European taxation matters.

Then you will hear Prof. Vogel who will speak of the tax encouragement given to investments, an important subject at this time of economic crisis. This afternoon, Prof. Hofstra, former Minister for Finance of the Netherlands will speak about net wealth taxes, and Mr. Airey will read a paper on the "taxation of companies in Europe, with special consideration of the effects of double taxation agreements". During the afternoon, we shall also have the honour of listening to M. Geens, the Belgian Minister for Finance.

Tomorrow's paper, written by Prof. Couturier, Vice-Rector of the University of Antwerp, will speak of interprofessional and international companies, i. e. the conditions of collaboration among tax consultants, accountants, lawyers and notaries in companies which either limit themselves to professionals of one country alone, or are constituted by professionals of different countries.

Each paper shall be followed by a short discussion on the main points and tomorrow the Congress shall be closed by a general discussion which, I hope, will lead to resolutions which will be the expression of a large consensus of all the members of our profession.

This Congress will thus be the expression of the European feeling of the tax consultants of all the countries of the Common Market and of their desire to collaborate in the construction of the European Community. They are aware, moreover, that this Community is the heart of Western democracy, and they know, as has recently been said by the German Minister Josef Ertl, that if this Community were not to be viable, it would mean the fall of democracy in Europe and perhaps even in the whole world. The tax consultants feel that the organisation of this present Congress was their duty as Europeans.

Welcoming Address at the Reception Given in the Town Hall in Honour of the Administrators of the C.F.E. and for the Honorary Guests of the Congress

Pierre Pflimlin
Mayor of the City of Strasbourg

Translated from French and German by Roselle Prill du Pradal

Ladies and Gentlemen,

I am pleased and honoured to welcome a delegation from your Confédération Fiscale. The very name of your Confédération stresses the importance which someone who is responsible for a city attaches to your profession, your competence, and your preoccupations, as they are also expressed in the programme of your congress, which I read with keen interest.

Tax questions are frequently a matter of concern in this city hall. Of course, we discuss mainly local taxes, and we are now entering the period of the year when we prepare our next budget. We are here responsible for two budgets, that of the City of Strasbourg and that of the urban community, and the crucial problem with which we are faced is to balance our budgets in such a way that the tax burden is not increased too much. Thus we are led to reflect upon the fiscal system of our country, and in order to be granted pardon by our tax payers who generally do not appreciate any increase in their taxes, we say to them: "It is not our fault, it is our tax system which is faulty". This is true to quite a large extent; so much so that the French government is preparing a municipal reform which shall also include a reform of municipal budgets. I do not yet know where this reform will take us; we have been waiting for reforms for a long time, but they do often bear resemblence to the sick who, in order to ease the pain, turn over on their other side; usually, this relief is only of short avail.

I say all this in the presence of the Trésorier Principal of the City of Strasbourg who is the most important person of this municipality. He represents the Ministry for Finance, and the Mayor is not entitled to spend even one penny without the approval of the Trésorier Principal. But I gladly extend my thanks to him, for he treats us with as much good will as is at all possible for a representative of the Ministry for Finance.

I understand that you also take an interest in the question of tax harmonization. This is a highly important subject. I remember that already some 20 years ago, when the foundations of the European Economic Community were being laid, this question of tax harmonization played an essential role. This was particularly true for France. At that time French negotiators stressed the importance of harmonizing all charges, e. g. social charges and also fiscal charges. Since then a few steps have been made in that direction. The value added tax which had been created in France, has been adopted by the other countries of the European Community. However, perfect uniformity is still a long way off, so that a lot of work remains to be done by you tax consultants and the specialists for fiscal questions. I feel that your profession will gain much in importance, because good dealings between the State and the tax payer depend to a large extent upon you. A knowledge of tax law, which is a highly complicated thing, is essential for the tax payer if he is to fulfil his tax obligations, all his tax obligations, but no more than his obligations. Specialists are often needed to determine the precise limits set down by law, which tax authorities may not surpass. I have been twice Minister for Finance. I have thus also considered this problem from the other side, but I have not changed my mind.

I think that those who sometimes suspect tax consultants of being the accomplices of fraudulent dealings are mistaken. Of course, as in all professions, there may be some black sheep. This exists in every profession. There are even some, so I hear, among politicians. I have never met any, but I hear that there are some ...

I had once the honour of welcoming here the Congress of Notaries, to mention another very honourable profession. The Congress was held following the arrest of one or two notaries in France. But this has in no way affected the every sincere respect which I hold for the profession of the notary.

Indeed, I think that you play a very important part in the interest of tax justice, and, in the final resort, in the interest of the State and also of local government, who benefit from taxes.

Monetary union is being widely discussed nowadays. The decisions which appear to have been prepared recently in Bonn give room for hope. We may be moving towards monetary union, but this union is not conceivable, and will not function properly, if the taxes of the different European countries remain so different and lead to distortions and inequalities in the tax burden. This brings me to a conclusion which I have made many times, Ladies and Gentlemen, and that is, that the unity of Europe must be sought at each of the various levels simultaneously. It is a serious mistake to believe that one can bring about unity in Europe in one field alone, in just one aspect of the problem. A total unity must be sought and brought about.

I express these thoughts in this hall which is one of the

cradles of Europe. In 1949, after the founding of the Council of Europe, at a time when the temporary Maison de l'Europe had not yet been built, it was in this room that the Members of the Committee of Ministers of the Council of Europe united for the first time. It was here, in this roo, that the very first debates took place, which enabled the foundation stones to be laid for this European construction which is not yet terminated. There is a long way yet to go; let us hope that it will rise little by little towards the sky. May it some day bear resemblence to our Cathedral and not to the tower of Babel.

Ladies and Gentlemen,

I have been informed that a number of the persons present come from the Federal Republic of Germany, perhaps also from Austria, and I would like to extend a warm welcome to them in the German language. It is for me always a great pleasure when guests come over from "the other side", as we say. Some decades ago "the other side" has had an unpleasant undertone. But now we think only of good neighbours, who have become friends. For us here in Strasbourg, for us Alsatians, the Franco-German reconciliation, the Franco-German friendship is a fundamental element as well as an objective of European unity. This was also the belief of my great friend Robert Schuman who was my mentor in the field of politics. He came from Lorraine; I come from Alsace; we shared the primary concern following World War II: "such a thing should never happen again". It was not sufficient that we merely sign peace treaties, as in the past. History has taught us that peace treaties are sometimes only scraps of paper, which are blown away by the wind storms of history. No, indeed, one must go further, much further. The idea of building a community was a stroke of genius. Not only making peace in the traditional sense, sitting down at a table and signing a peace treaty, maybe even against one's will, but forming together one grand family: that was the great concept which Robert Schuman had.

I extend to you all once more a warm welcome in the name of the City of Strasbourg, of course also to all the participants from the other countries of Europe, for Europe is not only an association between two countries, but a large family of peoples which one hopes shall become larger and larger. The Europe which we are now building is to be the Europe of free peoples. May fortune permit Europe to become in its entirety a Europe of freedom.

Welcoming Address

The Rt. Hon. Sir Derek Walker-Smith, Q.C., M.P.
President of the Legal Affairs Committee of the European Parliament, former Minister (United Kingdom), London

It is, Mr. President, a privilege and a pleasure for me to be associated with the inauguration of this First European Congress of Tax Consultants. It is indeed an auspicious and agreable occasion with the full promise of interesting and important deliberations. The importance of the occasion is reflected in the distinction of those who are to submit papers to its proceedings and not least in the fact that the proceedings are presided over by you, Sir, the eminent Président de la Confédération Fiscale Européenne, and that the Congress is to have the honour and good fortune to be addressed by so distinguished a member of the Commission as Commissioner Burke.

It would of course have been a particular pleasure for me to have the honour to be associated, as was intended, in this welcome with my distinguished friend, M. Pflimlin. He is, of course, distinguished in the broad context of the national life and politics of France, and his fame as mayor of the City of Strasbourg is legendary indeed. For many, the name of Strasbourg and Pflimlin are almost synonymous. Strasbourg is indeed fortunate in its mayor, as he in turn is fortunate in being chief citizen of this beautiful and historic city. And we who are privileged to pursue part of our labours here cherish each and all a warm affection for the City of Strasbourg and a profound appreciation of the unfailing kindness, courtesy and consideration of the people of Strasbourg and their mayor.

Now, Sir, it is abundantly apparent why M. Pflimlin should have been accorded the honour of an invitation to deliver a welcoming address on this historic occasion. But it is far less apparent why such an honour should have been extended to myself. After all, as lawyer and politician, I belong to what, I suppose, must be the two most unpopular callings in the world. Indeed, in earlier centuries, the first act of all successful revolutions was to put all the lawyers to death until, of course, in the French revolution, the lawyers found a way round that one and put themselves at the head of the revolution instead. As for the unpopularity of politicians, I recall, in earlier days, when I was Minister of Health in England, one of my ministerial colleagues entering into controversy with an eminent member of the medical profession - a thing which I quickly learnt not to do, after all doctors always have the last word anyway - and my ministerial colleague said to the doctor: "I suppose, there are two sorts of doctor, the young and experimental doctor who kills you off and the old and traditional doctor who leaves you to die." "Yes, Minister", said the doctor, "and there are two sorts of politician, those who are dead and those who ought to be." I hope that I will not be put in the second category in your judgement before I finish my short discourse.

In fact, I preside over a committee of lawyers and politicians in the European Parliament, and very nice people they are, I assure you, and very intelligent too. So I know that the invitation to me as Chairman of the Legal Affairs' Committee of the European Parliament, an invitation which I much appreciate, is a recognition of the important role that my committee can play in the liberalization of the national rules governing the liberal professions, a theme, Sir, to which you have fittingly referred in your eloquent opening address. We as a committee take a particular interest in the implementation of the Treaty provisions of freedom of establishment and freedom to provide services, and we are the Parliament's standing committee with primary responsability in this field. I was particularly pleased last year to see that after detailed discussions in Parliament and at the Council of Ministers a solution has been found to the problem of lawyers. The directive of the 12th March, 1977, to facilitate the effective exercise by lawyers, of freedom to provide services, marks a turning point in a profession where there are wide differences in national traditions on all aspects of professional activity. And I hope that a similarly satisfactory solution can be found for tax consultants.

You who are here today are concerned with taxation, a great and pervasive subject in this modern age. I was talking last month in Luxemburg - actually, Mr. President, in the absence of my friend, the Mayor of Strasbourg, I can refer to that other great city - I was talking last month with Chief Justice Warren Burger, the chief justice of the Supreme Court of the United States. And he reminded me of a passage in the great Maryland judgement of his famous predecessor, Chief Justice Marshal, referring to the unfettered nature of a government's right to tax. And in those memorable words, Chief Justice Marshal said this: "The only security against the abuse of this power is found in the structure of the government itself, in imposing a tax the legislator acts upon its constituents. This is in general a sufficient security against erroneous and oppressive taxation." Yes, to be sure, but - what is erroneous,- and what is oppressive? After all, tax law is notoriously complex and susceptible to error. And when we read in our history books, as we do, that the people of such and such a period grorned under the weight of oppressive taxation, we know that their burden of taxation was but slight compared with ours today. And so the citizen of today has very sensibly reinforced his protection by recourse to - I was going to say "Gentlemen like yourselves", but I am glad to see many charming ladies in this company - reinforced his protection by recourse to Ladies and Gentlemen like yourselves to guide him through the labyrinthine ways of taxation. And we are indeed grateful for the guidance of tax consultants. Another, more modern but very eminent American judge, Mr. Justice Earned Hand, said in a celebrated dictum: "Anyone may so arrange his affairs that his taxation shall be as low as possible; he isn't bound to choose that pattern which will best pay the State. There is not even a patriotic duty to increase one's taxation." Well, that judgement was nearly half a century ago when, of course, levels of taxation were much lower than they are today. Many years later, my wise and witty friend, Lord Diplock, said in the Court of Appeal in London: "There are few greater stimuli to human ingenuity than the prospect of avoiding fiscal liability. Experience shows that under this stimulus human ingenuity outreaches parliamentary pressures." Of course, it isn't a question of poachers and gamekeepers, as some people sometimes think. And legitimate avoidance will always fall far short of and be generically different from illegal tax evasion.

Everybody recognizes that the taxpayer has his duties, but he also has his rights and his right to assert those rights. And the State has its rights and its duties as well. And in the reconciliation of these complex rights and duties, you, Gentlemen, you, Ladies and Gentlemen, have a great and necessary part to play.

So we warmly welcome you here today for your deliberations on these important things. I referred a moment ago to an extract from the judgement of Chief Justice Marshal in the Maryland case. Let me conclude with another citation from the same judgement: "The power", said Chief Justice Marshal, "the power to tax involves the power to destroy, and the power to destroy may defeat and render useless the power to create."

The power to destroy, if that was true in 1819, how much truer must it be today, after more than a century and a half of increasing taxation. So let us then take heed, Ministers and Parliaments, Council and Commission, that we do not pursue courses that may defeat and render useless the power to create, and thereby arrest and put into retreat those dynamic impulses which can alone carry us forward to the continued progress and enhanced prosperity of our peoples.

So it is with a keen sense of my own inadequacy for the task, but with a sense nevertheless of pride and privilege that I have been entrusted with it, that I bid the Congress welcome this day and express to you each and all my best wishes for your sustained success and continued well-being in the good work in which you are engaged.

The Harmonization of Taxes in Europe

Richard Burke
Member of the Commission of the European Communities, Brussels

I greatly welcome this opportunity to tell you something about what we are trying to do in the European Community in connection with taxation.

In every modern state, taxation policy has become a preferred instrument of economic and social policy. Taxes are one of the decisive elements in economic and political life and must therefore play an important part in the development of the Community. There is at present no question of establishing a Community tax policy analogous to that which exists in the Member States. However, as you all know, plans for a European monetary system are now well advanced. This is a large step towards the fuller goal of economic and monetary union. Tax harmonization will play an important role in this process. Our aim is to remove impediments to competitive neutrality and to create the necessary conditions for the free movement of goods, services and persons throughout the Community.

VAT

Free movement of goods and services is obviously closely linked with questions of indirect taxation. As far as VAT is concerned, we can claim some considerable success. The latest important event in this area has been the adoption of the Sixth Directive, which establishes a uniform basis of assessment for VAT. There are admittedly a number of loose ends which are left to be tied up, but in principle this part of our task is now concluded. It is important to note that this Directive was introduced not just because of its effect upon the interchange of goods and services, but also because it was necessary to provide a basis for the financing of the Community budget. Because of delays by certain Member States in introducing the national legislation necessary to put the Sixth Directive into effect, this new method of providing funds for the Community from its own resources will not come into force until 1979.

Looking into the immediate future, we expect that the 8th Directive, concerning the reimbursement of VAT to non-resident taxable persons, will be adopted by the Council before the end of this year. The 7th Directive, on the application of VAT to second-hand goods and to antiques and so on (one of the loose ends I mentioned earlier), will not on the other hand be adopted before 1979.

Looking further into the future, the Commission has commenced work on studying the harmonization of VAT rates: how many rates should there be and which items will come within each rate band, if indeed there is more than one? This exercise will undoubtedly take some time. As further progress is made towards EMU we shall be able to decide upon a common rate, or common rates, and start moving towards their adoption throughout the Community.

Exemptions

Before turning to purely excise matters, I should like to mention a subject which concerns both VAT and excise, and which I expect has some personal interest for you in your daily lives. I am referring to tax-free allowances. You will be pleased to know that we expect the Council to adopt before the end of the year our proposals for increasing the exemptions for travellers, both between one Member State and another and between Member States and non-Member States, and for small packages of a non-commercial nature received from another Member State or from a third country.

EXCISES

In some Member States, consumer expenditure on goods subject to the "big 5" excises (that is, tobacco, oil, alcohol, beer and wine) is of the order of one-fifth of the total. The revenue alone from these taxes accounts for between 4 % and 13 % of consumer expenditure. These figures serve to show how important are the excises for the Community market.

Moreover, the excises are in general levied at very high rates, in many cases accounting for between a half and three quarters of retail price. Consequently, the excise industries are closely tied to the tax system in a number of crucial areas, such as pricing policy, their choice of product range, production methods, and so on.

At the present time, our chief attention is focused on the structure of the excise duties levied on alcoholic drinks. There are considerable differences in tax treatment between the Member States. Some practices are manifestly discriminatory. Given the high tax rates such differences and discriminations constitute serious obstacles to equal trading in these goods. Recently the Commission decided to take cases against a number of Member States before the European Court in Luxembourg in order to end discriminations in this area. However, to deal with the problem comprehensively will require uniform excise systems for these goods and we hope that this can be achieved by adoption by the Council of our harmonization directives next year.

DIRECT TAXATION

Let me say right away how particularly pleased I am to have the opportunity of explaining to this distinguished audience of experts the thinking behind the Commission's actions in this field and some of the difficulties that are being encountered, as well as our hopes for the future.

Evasion

It was last December that the Council, for the first time ever, adopted a Directive concerned with direct taxation matters. I am referring to the Directive providing for increased co-operation, in particular in the exchange of information, between the tax authorities of the Member States. There has been much concern that closer economic integration unfortunately brings with it increased opportunities for the abuse of its advantages through international tax avoidance and evasion. The new measure, which comes into full force throughout the Community on 1 January 1979, should bring important benefits in ensuring fair taxation in the interests of all.

Arbitration

The Commission is aware, nevertheless, that such a measure arouses fears of undesirable side-effects. For that reason, great care was taken to include most stringent secrecy provisions, to safeguard the legitimate interests of taxpayers. For that reason also, the Commission has put forward a proposal for a Directive on the elimination of double taxation in connection with the adjustment of transfers of profits between associated enterprises. For the first time in the world, this provides for an arbitration procedure where one Member State, applying its national law, increases the profits, for tax purposes, of an enterprise engaged in a transaction with an associated enterprise in another Member State which, for its part, does not make a corresponding downward adjustment.

What the Commission proposes is an extension of the existing mutual agreement procedure found in double taxation agreements, with the sole aim of ensuring that double taxation really is eliminated in all cases.

The general concept of the proposed Directive has attracted wide support. Let us all hope that the Council will demonstrate that the risk of overtaxation, at which it is aimed, is of as much political concern as is the danger of tax evasion.

I should now like to turn to the wider issues of direct tax harmonization.

Direct tax harmonization: general

If we are aiming at the creation of a real common market, which necessarily implies a high degree of economic and monetary union, we must remove barriers and distortions resulting from different tax regimes. We must in particular eliminate features of tax systems that prevent industry from organising itself on a European scale; that hinder the free movement of capital; and that work against neutrality in the conditions of competition.

Personal income tax

Now it is not our ambition to harmonize personal income tax in general, which is an important instrument of national policy and should be left to Member States even when the Community achieves a much higher degree of integreation than at present. But there are certain features of national income tax systems which may make it difficult for citizens of one Community country to work or settle in another - although such an effect was probably never intended. We are therefore examining the field of income tax in order to identify such obstacles or hindrances and see what can be done about them.

Mergers

The greater part of our activity is however, necessarily be concentrated upon the taxation of business enterprises and more especially companies. We are particularly concerned to make progress with matters that are already before the Council of Ministers. Some of them have indeed been before the Council for a very long time. I am thinking above all of the Proposal for a Directive on the common system of taxation to be applied to mergers taking place between companies of different Member States. This proposal was put forward early in 1969 - very nearly ten years ago - but the Council put it away in some forgotten pigeonhole where it has been gathering dust and cobwebs.

I am glad to tell you that this proposed Directive has been brought back to the light of day, dusted down and spruced up. Quite a lot of work has been going on and most of the technical problems have now been eliminated. The need is now for the political aspects to be dealt with at ministerial level.

Objections to Mergers Directive

I understand that some Member States see problems in the proposed Directive which are not directly connected with its immediate subject matter.

Link with Company Taxation Directive

It would be a pity if too much attention were paid to the suggestion that tax barriers to mergers and similar operations should not be removed until we have made greater progress towards the convergence of national tax systems - in particular, systems of company taxation, to which I shall turn in a moment. To take such an attitude is to suggest that nothing should ever be done unless perfection can immediately be achieved; and we all know that the practical effect is simply to block all progress.

Mitbestimmung

It would be a pity too if difficulties which really have nothing to do with tax at all but which nevertheless stand in the way of cross-frontier mergers - problems of worker participation are a familiar example - were to become entangled with the provisions of the proposed Directive. The problem of worker participation can only be solved in the context in which it belongs: the area of company law, where for example the committee under the chairmanship of Professor Goldman is already active. In so far as certain transactions, such as the contribution of assets by one company to another in return for shares, amounting to less than a merger in the strict sense, are already permitted under existing laws despite the effect they may have on worker participation, it is hard to see why the fair tax treatment so essential for Community-wide co-operation between enterprises should be refused.

Company Taxation Directive

More important, because of its wider scope and objectives, is the Proposal for a Directive on the harmonization of systems of company taxation and of withholding taxes on dividends, submitted by the Commission in 1975.

Existing CT systems

You are all, I am sure, very well aware of the extent, within the Community, of the differences between the various company taxation systems. We have, in one Member State or another, everything from the so-called classical system, with quite separate taxation of profits and dividends, to the complete elimination of this so-called economic double taxation. Most Member States come somewhere between these two extremes, with varying degrees of relief from the double taxation of distributed profits - relief which is given through one form or another of partial imputation, which means that part of the corporation tax charged on the company profits is given back, as a tax credit, to the shareholder receiving a dividend. This tax credit, however, is often not given to non-resident shareholders and in any case is never passed over from a subsidiary in one State through a parent in another State to the ultimate shareholder.

Need for harmonization of systems

Some people ask whether it is really necessary to harmonize these divergent systems. Would it not be better, they suggest, to try first of all to equalize the tax burdens on business enterprises in the different Member States by working towards a uniform definition of taxable profits - in other words, by harmonizing the tax base?

Let me say to these people: if we are serious about economic and monetary integration we cannot tolerate a situation in which a shareholder in one Member State receives the whole or part of the company tax back as a credit against his personal tax, whereas in another Member State he would receive a dividend which is in effect taxed twice. It is clear that a resident of a country with an imputation system who receives a tax credit as well as a cash dividend if he invests in a company in his own country, is not going to be very interested in investing in a company in another country where, under a classical system, distributed profits are taxed twice over and no tax credit is given. On the other hand, a resident of this second country receives an advantage if he invests across the frontier in a country with an imputation system, provided of course, that the tax credit is given across the frontier under a double taxation agreement. If the country with an imputation system does not grant the tax credit to residents or other Community countries, but only to its own residents, that is in itself an obvious discrimination.

This state of affairs distorts the flow of investment funds in the Common Market and can have adverse effects on essential parts of Community policy - regional policy for example and the transfer of resources. There is not much point in the Community developing policies intended to encourage investment in particular areas if the effect of the differing tax structures in the Member States is to pull the available funds even more strongly in a different direction. Thus, for example, a resident of a country with a full imputation system will always have the strongest inducement to invest in shares in his own country and not in another Member State.

Consider also the case of a parent company, resident in one Member State, which is considering establishing a subsidiary in another Member State. The fact that the taxation of a subsidiary's profits will never entitle the parent's shareholders to a tax credit, unless the subsidiary is in the same State, is bound to have an inhibiting effect on this most important form of capital export from highly industrialised to less industrialised Member States.

Harmonization of tax systems before tax base

The harmonization of the tax base is no alternative to the harmonization of the company taxation systems, because it would leave untouched these distortions in capital movements which come about precisely because the systems are unharmonized. Even if we could achieve complete harmonization of the tax base and complete uniformity of corporation tax rates tomorrow, we should not have achieved equalization of the tax burdens unless we had also harmonized the company taxation systems. Indeed, we should have made existing differences sharper, because with no difference in the tax rates the effect of giving part or all of the corporation tax back to shareholders as a tax credit in some countries, while not doing so in others, would be even more pronounced. The move towards a uniform measure of taxable profits has rather to come as the next step after harmonization of the systems and we are engaged in seeking an approach which will offer a prospect of progress in the present circumstances of the Community. We feel sure that this is the right order in which to tackle these problems.

Choice of system

The proposal we have put forward provides for the so-called partial imputation system, which has already been introduced, with a number of variations, in most Member States. We have therefore rejected not only the classical system, with its quite separate taxation of profits and dividends, but also the full imputation system, under which all the corporation tax on distributed profits is given back to shareholders. This latter system is now, of course, applied - in a rather special form - in the Federal Republic of Germany; and many who think we were right to turn our back on the classical system may wonder why we did not go right over to full imputation.

The answer is that to introduce such a system would in most Member States, and particularly those that at present have the classical system or only a mild degree of imputation, mean having to make a quite unacceptable choice between extravagantly high rates of corporation tax and substantial budgetary losses, which may have to be made good by other classes of taxpayers. Furthermore, it would be particularly expensive for countries which are not exporters of dividends, because they would lose a great deal of corporation tax across their borders in the form of tax credit.

I do not need to explain to this audience how the system chosen for taxing company profits and dividends affects the distribution policy of companies and their means of obtaining finance, as well as having a direct bearing upon the corporation tax rates and the withholding taxes upon dividends adopted by any particular State. These questions have been widely discussed within many Member States in recent years.

No widening of rate bands

Because we are concerned about Community-wide effects, particularly upon capital movements, it has been necessary for us to propose upper and lower limits for the rates of corporation tax and tax credit. Here and there the suggestion is voiced that we should open the rate bands so wide that we could accomodate both the German system and the classical system. If we were to adopt this course we should not have achieved any real harmonization. It would only be a pretence, a mere make-believe. The Commission being serious about European economic union, is convinced that the harmonization of company taxation systems within the Community must be a genuine harmonization. This does not mean rigid uniformity - flexibility is indeed at the present stage desirable and necessary - but it does mean a reasonably close convergence.

Importance for whole field of direct tax

The harmonization of company taxation systems has a fundamental importance for the whole development of direct taxation within the Community. Its link with the proposed Mergers Directive is a significant example. As I have mentioned earlier, some people take the view that the Mergers Directive will not produce its intended effects as long as the various Member States have widely different company taxation systems. Exaggerated as those fears are, there can nevertheless be no doubt that the mergers proposal makes more sense if it is to be followed by harmonization of the systems of corporate taxation. And if the Community institutions do not follow the lead which the Commission is giving here, the consequences for all further progress on direct taxation in accordance with Community goals will be serious and very far-reaching.

It is therefore extremely disappointing that this proposal, which is the most important single proposal for a Directive on direct tax harmonization, has been subject to delays and difficulties in the European Parliament since 1975. The favourable report of the Budget Committee, drawn up after a thorough and lengthy examination of the problems involved, was rejected by the plenary session in December of last year, for reasons which were never clearly stated. Since then, another parliamentary committee has been engaged in producing a new report. I have the impression that some people in Parliament think that because it is not easy to get a majority for any course of action in this area, no matter what it may be, it would be better simply to postpone all consideration of the subject for a few years. But nothing is gained by running away from the problem. The problem will, indeed, still be there and it will not get easier with the passage of time. Rather the reverse: if it is difficult now with nine Member States it will certainly not be any easier in a few years' time with a Community of twelve Member States. What is now thought of as a postponement for two or three years will then risk becoming indefinitely long. Members of Parliament should not let the present opportunity slip but should accept the responsibility of making a decision now. I must stress the risk we run: if the Community institutions lack the political will to undertake the most obvious step of bringing the company taxation systems into line, public opinion is likely to be puzzled by any other attempt at direct tax harmonization or EMU for that matter.

The Treatment of Capital Investments within the EC

Professor Dr. Horst A. Vogel
Steuerberater and Rechtsanwalt, Managing Director of the Institute 'Finanzen und Steuern', Bonn

Translated from German

I. Introduction to the problems

The six European States signatory to the Treaty establishing the European Economic Community [1], which was concluded in Rome in 1957, considered the objective of such a community to be the promotion of "a harmonious development of economic activities" [2] and a continuous and balanced economic expansion. The community was to be so established as to avoid major cyclical fluctuations and to maintain stability of price levels.

As a suitable measure for achieving these objectives, Article 2 of the EEC Treaty names the establishment of a common market, i.e. an integrated economic area within which conditions should be similar to those prevailing in a national domestic market. Next to the absence of customs frontiers, the main characteristic feature of such an economic area is the existence of uniform economic laws and regulations outlining the conditions for an economic system based on the principle of competition between individual business enterprises.

It is the task of the overall economic policy to devise those outlines - which include among other things all tax legislation directed towards revenue production - in such a manner that all persons or entities from the various Member States doing business may compete freely with one another, without any discrimination stemming from national laws.

In addition to providing for the establishment of a common market, Article 2 of the EEC Treaty calls for a progressive approximation of Member States' economic policies. Thus, alignment ist not to be restricted to a harmonization of the rules

---

1) dated 25 March 1957, BGBl Part II, p. 766

2) Art. 2 of the EEC Treaty

setting out general economic conditions, but is in addition to extend to those measures which directly affect the economic process. In the taxation field, this particularly refers to those additional measures which tend to be implemented in times of economic crises for the purpose of stimulating capital expenditures.

Much has been achieved, particularly in the customs and tariff fields since those early days when the objectives laid down in the EEC Treaty and the measures necessary to realize them were formulated. Good progress has also been made towards a harmonization of the bases on which value-added tax is imposed. What is called for now are efforts to tackle the harmonization of direct taxes. And it is exactly the divergent tax treatment of capital investments by the various States - made even more pronounced by steps taken in recent years to encourage them - that has brought about considerable differences in the burden of tax shouldered by business enterprises. The resultant inequality of competitive conditions is not compatible with Article 3 (f) of the EEC Treaty which calls for the institution of a system designed to ensure that competition in the common market is not distorted.

Moreover, they are an obstacle to the attainment of the goal set early in 1978 by EC President Roy Jenkins who, to overcome unemployment, demanded the creation of 15.5 million new jobs within the Community by 1985 [1]. The capital investments

1) Bulletin of the European Communities, No. 2/1978 page 7 et seq.

necessary for doing so should henceforth no longer be subjected to taxes the weight of which differs as a result of divergent national tax legislations. It is only by joint efforts and mutually dovetailed measures that medium -term stabilization of economic activity, coupled with an adequate and steady growth, can be brought about.

Distortions of competition resulting from differences in tax burdens are themselves reason enough for an attempt to bring in evidence the different tax treatment of capital investments and for discussions of the problems arising in connection with a comparison of the tax incidence of business enterprises. Moreover, harmonization of the rules of commercial law governing the determination of profits should lead to a first proposal for harmonization of the provisions under which profits are determined for tax purposes. Finally, the possibilities of harmonizing measures for encouraging capital investments will be discussed.

II. Differences in tax burdens on business enterprises within the EC

1. Ratios of tax revenue to GNP

A first approach to differences in tax burdens may be made by comparing total tax revenues accruing to the various individual States. However, a direct comparison of revenues in absolute terms necessitates conversion of the figures into one specific currency. Rates of exchange could serve as conversion ratios. But in any comparison extending over a number of years, the question of the date arises to which such rates of exchange should be related. Moreover, when it comes to the actual internal purchasing power of national currencies - and hence to the incidence of taxation within each State - rates of exchange are not very revealing. For comparisons of internal currencies, domestic purchasing power of the currencies concerned must be included in the conversion process [1]. It is only when based on representative consumption patterns that an international comparison of tax burdens becomes meaningful. But even here we come up against problems. First of all, there are a number of different statistical methods for determining purchasing power parities; and that poses the problem of the choice of a suitable conversion factor. Then, for each country to be included in the comparison, a conversion factor reflecting purchasing power must be taken into account in the calculations. If that were done, a comparison of tax burdens amongst the nine EC Member States would degenerate into a highly extravagent mathematical exercise.

All these difficulties do not crop up if you decide on an international comparison of taxation ratios. The reference figures are each country's GNPs to which the country's total revenue figure is related. The result, in percentage terms, is the country's "taxation ratio". A comparison of the taxation ratios within the EC reveals considerable differences in the size of the ratios [2]. They appear to indicate that Italy's tax burden is the lowest, her taxation ratio being 21,3 per cent for 1977. That country is followed by France (taxation ratio 24,9 per cent.) and the Federal Republic of Germany (taxation ratio 25,1 per cent.). In a mid-table position we find Belgium, the Netherlands and Great Britain. For Luxembourg, the ratio is already 35,4 per cent., for Denmark even 43,8 per cent. Thus, the difference between Italy, the country with the lowest ratio and Denmark with the highest is therefore 105 per cent.

---

1) Cf. Zeitel, G.: Gutachten über die Methodenwahl zur Durchführung eines Vergleichs der effektiven Steuerlast von Unternehmen in den Mitgliedstaaten der EWG, in: Commission of the European Communities (editor): Studies, Competition Series No. 7/1967, p. 12 et seq.

2) Cf. Annex, Table 1: Comparison of the "combined taxation and social security ratios" in the EC - 1977 -

If you consider the fact that in the Federal Republic of Germany an increase in the taxation ratio by one percentage point means provisionally depriving privatesector trade and industry of liquidity, otherwise available for private use, of no less than DM 13,000 million [1], an increase in taxation ratios may legitimately be claimed to be a fiscal drag on growth. Moreover, the large differences in ratios - which can also be detected by a comparison of the combined tax and social security ratios - can lead to distortions of competition. A detailed assessment of this, however, requires a differentiated comparison in addition to the global tax burden comparison. That would include, next to an analysis of tax systems by categories of tax, a study of the different legal rules, among which the treatment of capital investments in regard to valuation and depreciation are of importance in this context.

2. Structural differences in tax systems

a) Differences in the relationship between direct and indirect taxation

Even where taxation ratios are of equal size, tax systems must be taken to affect competition whenever the patterns of tax revenues differ [2]. A comparison of tax systems of the EC Member States based on the most recent available figures from 1976/77 reveals considerable differences [3].

1) Cf. Institut "Finanzen und Steuern", Brief 177, Bonn 1978, p. 12 et seq.

2) Cf. Report by the EEC Commission's Tax and Finance Committee 1962 (referred to as the "Neumark Report"), p. 20 et seq. Doc. 8070/2/XII/1962/5

3) In regard to the following figures cf. Annex, Table 2: "Tax receipts by categories of tax within the EC".

Luxembourg, for instance, derives more than 68 per cent. of her total tax revenue from direct taxes - which more recent nomenclature understands to cover taxes on income and property. That country is followed by Great Britain with 66 per cent., Denmark with 63.2 per cent. and the Federal Republic of Germany still with just under 62 per cent., France and Italy on the other hand rely more heavily on taxes on consumption, formerly termed indirect taxes. The latter two States receive more than half of their total tax revenues from indirect taxes. Conversely, their revenues from taxes on income and property are slightly more than 40 per cent.

It is to be assumed that the taxes on income and property weight more heavily on capital investments of a business enterprise, both in regard to their earning power and in regard to liquidity, than do indirect taxes . As far as the latter are concerned it can be expected that they are normally passed on in full in the price charged. What can therefore be said is that, all other conditions being equal, business enterprises are burdened all the less by taxes, the heavier the country concerned relies on indirect taxes. In all, business enterprises in those States have competitive advantages over such business enterprises as are burdened more heavily with direct taxes. Between the various categories of direct taxes within the EC there are again considerable differences in incidence. Not all countries impose the same categories of taxes. Thus, Belgium, France, Great Britain and Italy have no property tax at all while Denmark imposes property tax on individuals only. Ireland has repealed her wealth tax on individuals which she introduced in 1975 [1). Bodies corporate are not subjected to property tax except in the Federal Republic of Germany and Luxembourg.

---

1) Reported in Tax News Service, on 15 March 1978, published by the International Bureau of Fiscal Documentation.

In the Federal Republic of Germany, 8.9 per cent. of the 1977 total tax revenue was attributable to receipts from trade tax (Gewerbesteuer) which is imposed not only on business capital and business profits but also on aggregate wages and salaries paid. This "payroll tax", which appears to be an anachronism in these days of high underemployment, increases the cost of the factor "labour" and hence, at least in regard to the trend it generates, operates against efforts to reduce unemployment [1].

For 1976, Great Britain recorded no less than 12.6 per cent. of total tax revenue as stemming from the heavy taxes on land and buildings. In Italy and Belgium there are no taxes on land and buildings nor are there any trade taxes, whilst those taxes are of next to no importance at all in Denmark and the Netherlands.

What is of particular gravity, however, are above all the differences in income and corporation taxes. Whilst in France no more than 29 per cent. of total tax revenue stems from those taxes, the figure for Belgium is 58 per cent. Italy is the only EC Member State to place special emphasis on capital yields tax which in that country accounts for 13.9 per cent.

These sizeable differences are attributable to a number of factors [2]. First of all, the structures of the rate scales differ very considerably. In the Federal Republic of Germany, income tax is based on a rate scale derived from a formula whereas all other Member States have scales graduated according to income segments. At

1) Cf. Institut "Finanzen und Steuern", Brief 175: Die finanzwirtschaftlichen Probleme einer Aufhebung der Lohnsummensteuer, Bonn 1978

2) Cf. Annex, Table 3: "Scales of income tax rates in the EC".

national level, all scales begin with a flat-rate bracket, France having the lowest rate (5 per cent.) and Denmark the highest (36.4 per cent.). In all countries, that flat-rate bracket is followed by a zone of progressively increasing rates which ends at the top in an upper flat-rate bracket, the marginal rates of which vary to a great extent.

Corporation tax systems and rate structures are equally diversified [1]. Luxembourg and the Netherlands employ the "old-style" system of applying a standard scale of rates to a corporation's total profits and not providing for an integrated corporation tax system. Luxembourg's rates are on a progressively increasing scale. Partial credit against income tax of the corporation tax attributable to distributed profits is allowed in Belgium, Denmark, France, Great Britain and Ireland. The Federal Republic of Germany and, more recently, Italy as well, allow full credit against income tax of the tax borne by distributed profits, in which connection the Federal Republic employs the "split-rate" principle, i.e. where distributed profits are concerned it imposes the tax at a reduced rate of 36 per cent. rather than at the normal rate of 56 per cent.

In order to do away with this confusing variety of corporation tax systems, a variety which constitutes an obstacle to free circulation of capital, the Commussion of the European Communities drafted a directive for the harmonization of the systems and submitted it to the

1) Cf. Annex, Table 4: "Corporation tax systems in the EC - 1978".

Council as a proposal in 1975. It provides for the establishment of a system of partial credits and arrangements for the withholding of tax on dividends [1].

Once the European Parliament had, surprisingly, rejected the proposed directive in December 1977 [2], there is no more hope for a political agreement within the Council. But this failure to sway the European Parliament in the Commission's favour will cause the latter to prepare a new proposal, one that even countries with diametrically opposed tax systems - i.e. Luxembourg and the Netherlands on the one hand and Italy and the Federal Republic of Germany on the other - will be able to accept. In the long run, however, it would be desirable - and particularly so from the point of view of economic growth - to have a system accepted which provides for full credit being allowed against income tax of corporation tax paid on dividends.

b) Differences in valuation and depreciation of capital investments

Even differentiated studies of categories of taxes and scales of rates are by themselves not sufficient if you wish to arrive at a significant comparison of tax burdens on business enterprises in the various Member States of the European Community. What is of particular importance in this connection are the rules governing determination of profits for tax purposes and among these above all the rules on valuation and depreciation of capital investments. And, moreover, national investment incentive

---

1) Official Journal of the European Communities, No. C 253 of 5 November 1975, p. 2 et seq.

2) Cf. the paper by Hintzen, L.: Ein gangbarer Weg zur Harmonisierung der Körperschaftsteuer in der EG; in: Deutsche Steuer-Zeitung A 1978, p. 219 et seq.

measures must be included in the comparison [1].

All Member States, as a general rule, apply the "principle of nominal value" for the purposes of valuing items of fixed or current assets. This means that valuation proceeds from purchase price or production cost, less depreciation - i.e. the "historic costs".

It is only from time that there have been exceptions from that general rule in the various countries, viz. they occured only when a general new valuation of business assets was necessary to achieve an adjustment to the fair market value prevailing at a specific date. In connection with a reform of the currency system, in 1948, a large-scale new valuation of such nature took place in the Federal Republic of Germany for purposes of a so-called "DM Opening Balance Sheet" ("DM-Eröffnungsbilanz") [2].

---

1) The comparison of depreciation rules is primarily based on the following publications: Cahiers de droit fiscal international: Vol. LXI a, 1976; Vol. LXIII a 1977; Vol. LXII b 1977; Commission of the European Communities: Tax policy and investment in the European Community, Taxation Series 1975/1; ibid.: Report on the computation of business profits for tax purposes, Doc. No XVI/9/72, Brussels 1972 and the addendum to that Report, Brussels 1976; ibid.: Report on the computation of business profits for tax purposes, Brussles 1977; Mennel, A.: Internationaler Vergleich der steuerlichen Abschreibungen und Investitionsvergünstigungen, in: Recht der Internationalen Wirtschaft 1976, p. 321 et seq; Hausser, W./Müssener, J.: Steuerliche Abschreibung und Investitionsvergünstigungen im internationalen Vergleich, in: Internationale Wirtschaftsbriefe 1977, p. 709. Bundesministerium der Finanzen (editor): Informationsdienst zur Finanzpolitik des Auslands, No. 2/1977, No. 3/1977, No. 1/1978; Bracewell-Milnes, B./ Huiskamp, J.C.L.: Investment Incentives, Deventer 1977.

2) Ordinance concerning the Opening Balance Sheet in Deutsche Mark and Capital Re-organization of 21 August 1949, Gesetzblatt der Verwaltung des Vereinigten Wirtschaftsgebietes 1947 - 49, p. 279.

In Italy, "historic costs" were subjected to an upward adjustment for the period preceding 1974 by application of a revaluation factor [1]. In its Financial Laws for 1977 [2] and 1978 [3], France, too, allowed a revaluation of certain fixed assets by application of an inflation coefficient. Any gain derived from such revaluation was allowed to be allocated to a tax-free reserve.

At present the "principle of nominal value" is under discussion and particularly so in countries with high rates of inflation. The problems arising in this context will be dealt with later in this paper in connection with the efforts to harmonize the rules of commercial law governing the determination of profits.
A peculiarity should be noted in regard to Luxembourg and the Federal Republic of Germany. In those two States, fixed assets subject to wear and tear may be written down to a "going concern value" ("Teilwert"). This is understood to mean the value which a purchaser of the business enterprise as a whole would attribute to the individual asset when apportioning the overall purchase price, always provided that he would continue to carry on the business.

Whereas a comparison of valuation principles still reveals a large measure of conformity, there are material differences in regard to depreciation procedures. What is called for is a clarification of national rules, particularly in regard to the following questions:

---

1) Law of 2 December 1975, No. 576; cf. also Mayr, S.: Italien - Neubewertung des Anlagevermögens, in: Intertax 1976/2, p. 46 et seq.

2) Loi de Finances pour 1977, Journal Officiel, 30 December 1976.

3) Loi de Finances pour 1978, Journal Officiel, 31 December 1977.

1. What fixed assets may be written off?
2. Is there a statutory obligation to take depreciation and to what extent may untaken depreciation be recovered in subsequent assessment periods?
3. As from what date may depreciation commence?
4. Differences in methods and rates of depreciation.
5. Are there, in addition to normal depreciation, other more generous tax measures to encourage capital investments?

Now, this speech is not intended to give a highly detailed account of the situation in each individual State in regard to the above-mentioned questions. What is really important is that it describes the problems which will arise in future negotiations on harmonization. For this purpose, an attempt will be made to outline the range over which the differences are spread.

The answer to the question as to whether, and if so, to what extent tax legislation in Member States allows depreciation of a kind that results in tax reductions is one that at present is still more or less the same for all States. In all EC countries, movable and immovable fixed assets subject to wear and tear are depreciable. It is only in regard to intangible assets that differences are apparent. Patents may be written off in all States, and other intangibles - for instance, the goodwill of a business - are depreciable especially in cases where they were acquired for a consideration.

Alone the question whether there is an obligation, under tax legislation, to take depreciation and to what extent untaken depreciation may be recovered in later periods calls for highly divergent answers. In Belgium, Denmark, Great Britain and Ireland, as a general rule, there is no obligation to write off assets. Untaken depreciation may be recovered in later assessment periods though in some cases not before the asset in question is disposed of by the business. In Germany, Italy, Luxembourg and the Netherlands there is a statutory obligation to take depreciation each year. If a taxpayer fails to take depreciation the tax authorities in Germany, ex officio, make corresponding deductions when determining the taxpayer's profit for tax purposes. It is only on Italy that recovery of untaken depreciation is possible whenever the asset concerned is utilized in the business beyond the normal useful life it has in the particular line of business. In France, assets purchased or produced after 31 August 1965 may, if depreciation was not taken in years of loss, be recovered in later assessment periods provided that they are reflected in book values. If not so reflected, depreciation may not be recovered.

And also the question as to the date on which the taxpayer may commence to take depreciation calls for differing answers. While in Belgium and the Federal Republic of Germany, the relevant date is that when the asset was purchased or produced, depreciation may not be taken in the other States before the date on which the asset is put to use in the business. During the year in which the asset was purchased or put to use, depreciation may be taken at the full annual rate or else it is taken on a pro rata temporis basis.

A comparison of depreciation methods and rates reveals the following: [1)]

1) Cf. Annex. Table 5 "Depreciation for tax purposes in the EC - 1978".

The main method used in all Member States is the straight line one where purchase price or production cost is apportioned over the period of useful life customarily attributed to the asset in the particular line of business.

Buildings used for business purposes are subject to straight line depreciation in all Member States, though rates of depreciation and the periods of useful life vary considerably. In Great Britain and Ireland, industrial buildings are written off after no more than 13 years of use - the initial rate of depreciation alone coming to 54 per cent. of the overall purchase price or production cost. Ireland is even planning to allow, in future, depreciation of up to 100 per cent. for the first year.

Next to the Netherlands, the Federal Republic of Germany attributes the longest periods of useful life to buildings. Depreciation may be taken over a period of 50 years at a rate of 2 per cent. of the purchase price or production cost. Application of a higher rate of depreciation is possible only if the building's actual economic lifetime is less than 50 years. The tax authorities normally accept 33 1/3 years as a period of useful life, customary in the line of business, for buildings used by the business, in other words, they allow a depreciation rate of 3 per cent. per annum.
In addition, there is available what is known as a combined "straight-line/declining balance" method of depreciation: buildings produced after 31 August 1977 may be depreciated during the first 12 years at a rate of 3.5 per cent. of the relevant costs, in the following 20 years at a rate of 2 per cent. and in the remaining 18 years at a rate of 1 per cent.

Even where movable items of fixed assets subject to wear and tear are involved, basic depreciation follows the straight line method. In addition, the tax laws of eight States also allow declining balance depreciation to be applied. Only

Italy does not permit this method to be used. The procedural details are just as varied as the level of the rates of depreciation and the lengths of periods of useful life allowed as customary in the line of business concerned. In two Member States, periods of useful life are only of minor importance. In Great Britain, the initial rate of depreciation is optional and can be anything up to 100 per cent of the purchase price or production cost. If a lower rate is written off during the first year, the remainder is depreciated under a pooled declining balance method at an annual rate of 25 per cent. The Republic of Ireland allows not only depreciation in the first year at an optional level, but permits also optional rates during the following years up to an aggregate of 100 per cent.

Italy's and Denmark's positions are opposites. Italy allows only the straight line method whereas Denmark permits only a pooled declining balance method at a rate of 25 per cent. The other Member States link the declining balance rate with the straight line rate in that they, as a rule, allow the former to be double, or two and one half times, the straight line rate, with a maximum fixed at 20 to 25 per cent. of the book value. Only Belgium allows genuine double rate depreciation equal to two times the straight line rate without any restriction to a specific percentage of the book value. A switch from one method to another in States where more than one method is in existence, is mostly allowed only if the declining balance method is to be abandoned in favour of the straight line one.

In most Member States there are no statutory rules on depreciation on the basis of asset utilization. That method is customary only in France, Luxembourg, the Netherlands and Germany.

The last important point to be described is in how far there are measures to encourage capital investments over and above existing depreciation facilities.

National measures and the way they are designed are once again varied.

Accelerated depreciation is a widespread method under which the costs of capital investments may be written off at a more rapid rate than that corresponding to the period of useful life customary in the line of business. The usual full depreciation during the first year allowed in Great Britain and Ireland comes under this heading just as the accelerated depreciation does which Italy allows for movable assets in the first year at a rate of 15 per cent. of the purchase price or production cost, in addition to the normal annual depreciation rate. In Belgium and France, capital investments for research and development are encouraged by means of accelerated depreciation facilities. Investment allowances, which permit a certain percentage of the purchase price or production cost to be deducted from the tax base, are customary in five Member States, but their objects and procedural details differ.

In Luxembourg, an investment tax credit is allowed to be deducted from the amount of tax payable. In Germany, the "Stability Law" [1] authorizes the Government to issue regulations, without prior approval by Parliament, likewise allowing - in the event of a threat of economic imbalance - the deduction from the amount of income or corporation tax payable of 7.5 per cent. of the purchase price or production cost of capital goods, such deduction being restricted to one year.

---

1) Sec. 26 of the Law to Promote Stability and Growth of the Economy (Gesetz zur Förderung der Stabilität und des Wachstums der Wirtschaft) of 8 June 1967 (BGBl I p. 582).

To encourage capital investments, Denmark permits the allocation to an investment reserve of up to 25 per cent. of annual profits. The amount of the allocation must be deposited in a blocked account and must within 12 years be used for a preliminary depreciation of qualifying investments.

Over and above these purely tax measures, Germany grants investment premiums from 7.5 to 15 per cent. in respect of capital investments used for the production and distribution of energy or used for research and development purposes or used for economic development in certain regions [1].

If for purposes of comparing the tax treatment of capital investments within the EC we place side by side depreciation facilities, including general accelerated depreciation facilities, investment allowances and deductions from tax, other than those restricted to specific periods of time, the following picture emerges [2]: Thanks to the system of free depreciation, capital investments are written off most rapidly in Great Britain and Ireland. A machine with a useful life of ten years is written off after the lapse of three years, as follows, in the other Member States:

- in Italy by 75 per cent.
- in Denmark and France by 66 per cent.
- in the Federal Republic of Germany by 58 per cent.
  and
- in the Benelux countries by 49 per cent.

---

1) The Investment Premium Law, as amended by 3 May 1977; a further amendment is being prepared envisaging premiums of 15 per cent. up to a maximum of DM 500,000 to encourage capital investments for research and development purposes and the production and distribution of energy; cf. for most recent news: Bericht des Finanzausschusses zum Entwurf eines Gesetzes zur Änderung des Investitionszulagengesetzes, BT-Drucks 8/1731 of 5 May 1978.

2) Cf. Annex, Table 6: General tax benefits offered in regard to expenditure on capital investments in the EC - 1978 -.

After the lapse of 7 years, it is already written off by the following percentage figures:

- in Belgium, Denmark, France and Italy by about 90 per cent.
- in the Federal Republic of Germany by about 87 per cent., and
- in Luxembourg and the Netherlands by no more than 80 per cent.

3. The problematical nature of comparisons of the tax incidence on business enterprises in the EC

Neither a comparison of the ratios of tax revenues to GNP, nor the comparison of the different tax revenues themselves, nor an analysis of the valuation and depreciation provisions seen in conjunction with more generous measures to encourage capital investments, are by themselves sufficient to make the actual tax burden on business enterprises of the various Member States comparable. What must actually be done is to try and bring into relation the different depreciation systems to the scales of tax rates concerned.
Calculations [1)] resulting in such relations reveal the fact that the tax burden on buildings used for business purposes is heaviest in the Federal Republic of Germany, in the Netherlands and in Luxembourg, whereas the burden is much lighter in Ireland, Great Britain and Italy. The ranking is similar when it comes to the tax burden on movable items of fixed assets. Business enterprises in the Federal Republic, the Netherlands and Luxembourg shoulder the largest burden, while those in Great Britain and Ireland shoulder a much lesser one, thanks to the initial depreciation facilities.

---

1) Cf. the calculations made by Snoy: Taxes on direct investment income in the EEC, A legal and economic analysis, New York-Washington-London 1975, particularly p. 84 et seq.; Dreyer/Lühmann: Auswirkungen der Unterschiede steuerlicher Abschreibungsmöglichkeiten auf die Wettbewerbslage der Unternehmen in den EG-Ländern, in: Finanzrundschau 1978, p. 83 et seq.

However, such calculations are by no means lacking in problems. First of all, the calculations proceed from the assumption that capital produces an equal yield in all countries, which is certainly not the case. On the other hand, such comparisons must, in addition to income and corporation taxes, also include those taxes which are not based on income or profits. Furthermore, if it were practicable also to include all possibilities which individual business enterprises may have to pass on certain tax burdens, the result would be much more revealing.
But it is at this point that economists come up against hitherto unsolved problems. Nevertheless, what has become apparent is the fact that the multiplicity of the disclosed differences results in competitive disadvantages for those business enterprises which have their registered offices in countries imposing heavy tax burdens. Moreover, this weakens the competitive position of the whole EC as an integrated economic area in its business dealings with third countries. The existence, however, of these manifold differences must not mislead one to expect the accomplishment in a foreseeable time of an alignment of the Member States' categories of taxes, their scales of tax rates, and also of their rules for determining profits.
So what is needed is at least to find a starting point for tackling the whole range of harmonization problems, viz. to agree on the "lowest common denominator". The first attempt to achieve harmonization might be in the field of determining profits for tax purposes.

III. Harmonization of the provisions on the determining of profits for tax purposes

1. Prevalence of the rules of commercial law in determining profits for tax purposes

Any harmonization of the provisions on the determining of profits for tax purposes must be preceded by an answer to the question of the extent, if any, to which the profit determination rules of commercial law come to bear in this connection in Member States. This question has become even more weighty since the adoption in July 1978 by the Council of the European Communities of the Fourth EC Directive on the harmonization of the rules of commercial law governing the accounts of certain companies with limited liability, which Directive will be explained briefly later in this paper with regard to the objective it pursues and the measures it envisages.

In the Federal Republic of Germany and in Luxembourg, the principle that the provisions of commercial law prevail in determining profits for tax purposes (hereinafter referred to as "prevalence principle") [1] is strictly observed. The commercial balance sheet, which must be drawn up with due regard to generally accepted accounting principles, is modified under the provisions of tax law and thereupon taken as a base to which the scale of tax rates is applied. There is no independent balance sheet purely for tax purposes; the principle applied is that any obligation under commercial law to carry certain items on the assets or liabilities side of the balance sheet must likewise be observed when determining profits for tax purposes. Equally,

---

1) Cf. Knobbe-Keuk, B: Bilanz- und Unternehmenssteuerrecht, Cologne 1977, p. 11 et seq.

any prohibition under commercial law against carrying certain items on the assets or liabilities side of the balance sheet is authoritative in regard to the figures entered in the balance sheet for tax purposes. However, whenever the entering in the balance sheet of an item as an asset is optional under commercial law, it is obligatory for tax purposes. The "prevalence principle" also applies in matters of valuation. Where, for tax purposes, an option is allowed on a point of valuation, it is the figure entered in the commercial balance sheet that must be adhered to, unless tax legislation prescribes something different. In the other seven countries belonging to the EC there is no such wide prevalence of the commercial balance sheet in the determination of profits for tax purposes. Nevertheless, the commercial balance sheet is taken as a starting point in all States. As far as the author is aware, none of the Member States have separate rules under which the determination of profits for tax purposes would be accomplished with absolutely no regard being had to the commercial balance sheet. [1] That is why the effects of the Fourth EC Directive on the harmonization of the rules of commercial law governing annual accounts will also have to be observed in all Member States in connection with the determination of profits for tax purposes.

2. Objectives of the Fourth EC Directive and its tax consequences

The Fourth EC Directive on the harmonization of the rules of commercial law governing annual accounts [2] within the European Communities pursues the following objectives:

- To establish equivalent legal requirements for companies

---

1) Cf. Mennel, A.: Die Steuersysteme in EWG-Staaten, EFTA-Staaten und in den USA, second edition, Herne/Berlin 1974.

2) Cf. Official Journal of the European Communities, No. L 222 of 14 August 1978, p. 11 et seq.

that are in competition with one another as regards the extent of the financial information to be published.
- To ensure that a true and fair view of a company's assets and liabilities, financial position and profit or loss is given, so as to protect members and justified claims by third parties.
- To provide for the comparability of annual accounts.
- To ensure that annual accounts are readily accessible.

These objectives are to be achieved by means of the coordination of national provisions concerning the presentation and content of annual accounts, the coordination of valuation methods, and publication of these accounts in respect of certain companies with limited liability. For this reason, the Directive prescribes a detailed mandatory layout for balance sheets and profit and loss accounts. In addition, notes on the accounts must be prepared, the essential purpose of which is to supply information on the valuation methods used and on conversions into local currency. Furthermore, an annual report must be drawn up which must include a fair review of the development of the company's business and of its position. In future, valuation for purposes of annual accounts is to be governed by standardized general principles in all EC Member States. Next to the principle of consistency in the application of valuation methods, Article 31 above all codifies the principle of prudence: only profits made at the balance sheet date may be included, while account must be taken of all liabilities and potential losses as are foreseeable at the balance sheet date and have arisen in the course of the financial year concerned or of a previous one ("imparity principle").

The "principle of balance sheet continuity" means that the opening balance sheet of each financial year must correspond to the closing balance sheet for the preceding financial year.

The components of asset and liability items must as a general rule be valued separately by application of the purchase price principle. However, Article 33 (1)(a) offers the alternative of valuation by the replacement value method.

The advocates of valuation with reference to replacement costs very properly draw attention to the fact that in times of increasing currency erosion valuation by the historic cost method results in the balance sheet's showing fictitious profits which do not truly reflect the profit or loss position of the business and may lead to real-asset losses. This danger might, however, be mitigated if countries with a high rate of currency erosion could from time to time implement revaluation schemes - similar to those implemented by France and Italy in recent years. Departures from valuation under the "nominal value principle" could thus be no more than temporary, i.e. always when persistently high rates of inflation make revaluation absolutely necessary. The advantage of revaluation from time to time is that on the one hand it avoids, whenever high rates of inflation prevail, the emergence of fictitious profits over a multi-annual period, and on the other hand it restricts the danger of a surrender to inflation inherent in a general departure from the nominal value. The purchase price or production cost or, if valuation is based on Article 33 the replacement cost, of fixed assets with limited useful economic lives must be reduced by value adjustments so calculated as to ensure a systematic write-off of such assets over the period they are in use (Article 35). However, no specific method of depreciation is prescribed, so that in this respect no harmonization has been achieved. Nor does the Fourth Directive contain anything on the level of depreciation rates.

Value adjustments may be made in respect of financial fixed assets to the effect that they are valued at the lower figure to be attributed to them at the balance sheet date. Where fixed assets are concerned, such value adjustments are obligatory if it is expected that the reduction in their value will be permanent. However, no adjustments may be made in respect of temporary reductions of the value of fixed assets [1]. This restricts the possibility of creating hidden reserves. Contrary to the rule laid down in the German Company Law (Aktiengesetz), a corresponding upward adjustment must be made if the reasons for the downward adjustment cease to apply. This obligation to make an upward adjustment in value is once again designed to restrict the possibility of creating hidden reserves. If fixed assets are the subject of exceptional value adjustments for taxation purposes alone, the amount of the adjustments and the satisfactory reasons for making them must be indicated in the notes on the accounts.

Formation expenses must be included under "Assets" where this is authorized under national law. They must be written off within a maximum period of five years. As long as this has not been done, no distribution of profits may take place unless general reserves and profits brought forward are at least equal to the amount of the expenses not written off (Article 34).

The same applies to such costs of research and development as are required by national law to be included under "Assets". Derogation may, however, be permitted in exceptional cases. The reasons for them must be disclosed in the notes on the accounts (Article 37 (1)).

---

1) Section 154 (2) of the German Company Law (Aktiengesetz) allows value adjustments in cases where the reduction in value is merely temporary.

Goodwill, if acquired for valuable consideration, must be written off systematically over a period of five years. A limited period of more than five years is allowed only if it does not exceed the probable useful life of the assets (Article 37 (2) read in conjunction with Articles 9 and 10).

The general rule is that current assets must be valued at purchase price or production cost. If their market value is lower, corresponding value adjustments must be made. Valuation at the lower value must be discontinued, if the reasons for which the value adjustments were made have ceased to apply. If exceptional value adjustments are made solely for taxation purposes, the reasons for making them must be disclosed in the notes on the accounts. Under Article 40, Member States may permit the purchase price or production cost of stocks of goods of the same category, and of all fungible items [1], including investments, to be calculated, at the company's option, either on the basis of weighted average prices or by the "first in, first out" (FIFO) method or by the "last in, first out" (LIFO) method or by some other similar method.

---

1) Cf. subparagraph 2 of Section 40 (4) of the German Commercial Code.

3. More intensive harmonization needed of provisions on determining profits for tax purposes

The explanatory valuation rules derived mainly from a dynamic approach to balance sheet matters [1] are largely commensurated with the rules governing accounting in Germany and the U.S.A. Generally speaking, uniform application of the Fourth EC Directive could very well result in its objectives being achieved, viz. establishing equivalent legal requirements for companies, and ensuring that annual accounts give a true and fair view of a company's assets and liabilities, its financial position and its profit or loss. But it is exactly this uniform application which is placed in jeopardy by a multitude of national and company-related options. Alone in the field of valuation and entering items as assets in the balance sheet there are 27 options [2]. These options reveal the highly divergent positions held by Member States [3], so that one can expect there will, neither now nor in future, be any complete comparability of annual accounts.

---

1) Schmalenbach, E.: Dynamische Bilanz, 17th ed., Cologne/ Opladen 1966; regarding the significance of a dynamic approach to balance sheet matters cf. Knobbe-Keuk, B.: Bilanz- und Unternehmenssteuerrecht, loc. cit. p. 9 et seq.

2) Cf. for details the mimeographed manuscript by H. Jonas: Zur Problematik der 4. EG-Richtlinie, Ludwigshafen 1978, p. 10 et seq.

3) Particularly the reserve entered by the German Delegation regarding Article 35 - valuation with reference to replacement costs - which nearly prevented the Directive from being adopted.

However, the Fourth EC Directive can nevertheless at least serve as a starting point for the necessary harmonization of the rules on the determination of profits for tax purposes. If the rules on the layout of annual accounts and on the valuation principles were, throughout the EC territory, to form the basis of those balance sheets which are to be drawn up for tax purposes, there would be no need again to waste many years in an attempt to reach agreement on what should be the basis for determining profits for tax purposes. In order to avoid an inflation of national tax laws caused by introducing the provisions due to be harmonized, it would appear reasonable to lay down by law in all EC Member States that the principle of prevalence of the commercial balance sheet in connection with the determination of profits for tax purposes [1]. In that event, all rules of commercial law requiring certain items to be, or preventing them from being, carried as assets or liabilities in the balance sheet would also apply for tax purposes.

However, in regard to certain problems a renewed attempt would nevertheless have to be made to reach agreement on a further harmonization of rules of tax law.

The purchase price or production cost (or the replacement value if valuation is governed by Article 33) of fixed assets with limited useful economic lives must be reduced by value adjustments calculated to write off the value of such assets systematically over their useful economic lives (Article 35). This rule, consequently, does not

1) In the Federal Republic of Germany the prevalence principle is laid down in Section 5 (1) of the income Tax Law.

tie down business enterprises to apply a specific depreciation method and they are thus able to choose a depreciation method suited to the operational conditions surrounding their business. What should be noted is that some national legislators are restricting the scope of depreciation for tax purposes to less than what commercial law allows. A rule for harmonizing tax law in this field should, in regard to depreciation methods, adopt the options allowed under commercial law. Those Member States whose rules of depreciation for tax purposes go beyond those laid down in commercial law would have to adapt their tax provisions to the provisions of the Fourth EC Directive. Thus, for instance, one might contemplate introducing EC-wide a tax rule which would base depreciation on the straight line method but would also allow application of the declining balance method up to a maximum rate equal to treble or quadruple the straight line rate. Such a solution would comply with the rule that the value of assets must be written off systematically over such assets' useful economic lives, while not narrowing the scope within which business management is wont to make its decisions.

Next to calling for a systematic write off of the value of assets, Article 35 lays down the obligatory rule that if it is expected that the reduction in the value of a fixed asset will be permanent, such asset must be valued at the lower figure. However, valuation at the lower figure may not be continued if the reasons for which the value adjustments were made have ceased to apply. Such an obligation under commercial law to rectify previous downward value adjustments might, if the principle of prevalence of the commercial balance sheet in matters connected with determining profits for tax purposes is applied result in an increase in taxable income by a margin actually constituting "unrealized profits". The taxation of unrealized profits would, however, run counter to the principle of prudence and would create a liquidity problem for business enterprises. Consequently, provision would have to be made to ensure that any profits resulting from such a compulsory rectification of previous value adjustments would be allowed to be placed in a tax free reserve.

Article 40 leaves it to the Member States' discretion to permit, where stocks of goods of the same category are concerned, the purchase price or production cost to be calculated for purposes of commercial law either on the basis of weighted average prices or by the LIFO or the FIFO method. This rule, which is to be welcomed from the point of view of business usage, should be adopted in the course of the harmonization of the rules on determining profits for tax purposes.

A further problem arises in connection with the valuation of holdings in affiliated undertakings. Pending subsequent coordination, Member States are allowed by Article 59 to introduce valuation of such holdings by the "equity method". The purchase price of holdings in affiliated undertakings is increased or reduced by the profits or losses realized or sustained by the affiliated undertaking, calculated according to the percentage of capital held.

Hence, a parent company's share in its subsidiary's profits is already deemed to have been received by the former at the point of time when it accrues to the latter. When the subsidiary actually distributes such profits, the book value of the holdings concerned is reduced by a sum equal to the distribution and is therefore treated as being neutral for tax purposes.

If the subsidiary, rather than distributing the full dividend to its parent company, retains and ploughs back a portion thereof, the result will be that the parent company will show an unrealized profit in its balance sheet and insofar will violate the principle of valuation by purchase price or production cost (Article 32) and also the provision prohibiting the inclusion in the balance sheet of unrealized profits (Article 31 (1) (c)). In order to avoid a distribution of such profits shown but not realized, they must be placed in a reserve which may not be distributed to shareholders.

The result of valuation by the equity method is that it offers an improved insight into the parent company's assets. When translating the directive into rules of tax law, the following should apply:

The reserve to be shown in the commercial balance sheet must remain tax free since otherwise there would be a case of taxing unrealized profits to the parent company.

Another point to be mentioned is the possibility, hitherto unknown to German commercial and tax law, of creating provisions to cover certain future expenses and charges. So far, the only provisions allowed under commercial and tax law have been those which were clearly in the nature of a debt. This sets the Federal Republic apart from her European neighbours to whom such a narrow concept of provisions is alien. Permissibility of the creation of such provisions for certain future expenses and charges (e.g. cost of preparing annual accounts) under German commercial and tax law as a result of the alignment of legal systems would indeed be welcome.

IV. Harmonization of capital investment incentives within the EC

1. Objectives of capital investment incentives

Next to those measures which relate to depreciation rules and which serve overall economic policies, all EC Member States pursue wider objectives of varying kinds which make a differentiation of capital investment incentives necessary [1].

On the one hand, all States encourage investments in regions where economic weakness stems from an unfavourable geographical location. Next to these, sectoral encouragement measures should be mentioned which are either implemented in the form of adaption or maintenance aids to industries highly jeopardized by structural changes, or are designed to promote such specific industries as are of vital importance to the equilibrium of the economy as a whole. Two examples worth mentioning are safeguarding the supply of energy or selective encouragement measures to promote research and development.

Furthermore, capital investments serving environmental purposes are encouraged throughout the territory of the EC with a view to improving not only quantative economic growth but also the conditions of life.

1) In view of the multitude of different provisions, reference is made to the EC Commission's comprehensive reports, especially: Tax Policy and Investment inthe European Community, loc. cit., and: Report on the Computation of Business Profits for Tax Purposes, loc. cit.

2. Critical assessment of individual investment incentives - Possibilities for harmonization -

If investment incentives designed to increase earning power should become necessary in order to boost either the economy as a whole or certain sectors thereof - and that might be particularly called for in the fields of energy production and distribution, of research and development, and of improving the economic structures of certain regions - a system of special depreciation allowances or of investment premiums would be suitable devices to achieve this object.

Special depreciation allowances have a disadvantage in that the full benefit from them can be derived only by business enterprises making a good profit; moreover, their effect differs according to the progressive increases in the table of tax rates. That is why the trend is becoming apparent within the Community to give preference to investment payments or investment premiums. The most recent example is that of the Netherlands where the entire incentive system was switched from special depreciation allowances to investment premiums.

Such investment premiums could either be granted in the form of an investment tax credit or else in that of an investment payment in no way related to the tax payable by the business enterprise concerned. The advantage of direct investment payments is that they benefit all business enterprises alike whilst tax credits operate to the disadvantage of exactly those business enterprises which pay no tax at all because they are running up a net loss. Nevertheless, what might be considered is whether a tax credit to be granted in respect of capital investments should be allowed not only as a deduction from the amount of income or corporation tax payable [1] but also as a deduction from value added tax whenever the business enterprise concerned has incurred a net loss. For this purpose, the advantage deduction figure would be increased by a percentage rate related to the purchase price or to production cost. If this particular method of deducting the premium from the tax amount payable were adopted, there would largely be no need for a special procedure of prior claims and approvals as is required if the investment payment method is applied. Whether or not the conditions, to be laid down by the legislative bodies, for deducting the premium from the tax amount payable were complied with could be determined in connection with the business enterprise's assessment for value added tax. Such a measure would constitute an additional and prompt, and hence promising, form of liquidity aid and would offer an extra improvement of earning power for all business enterprises without necessitating the interposition of a protracted claim and approval procedure [2].

An EC-wide harmonization of procedures for, and rates of, investment premiums might perhaps be brought about in the fields of research and development and in the energy field.

---

1) The German Income Tax Law provides that in the event of a threat of imbalance of the national economy a regulation - not requiring prior approval by Parliament - may be issued, under which a 7.5 per cent. tax credit is temporarily allowed to be deducted from the income or corporation tax payable by the business enterprises concerned.

2) For a time, France used such a form of deduction from value added tax as an investment incentive: Law No. 75-408 of 29 May 1975; Article 2 - I of Law No. 75-853 of 13 September 1975.

A harmonization of incentives for regional or sectoral measures to improve economic structures would, however, be neither practicable nor desirable on account of the completely different problems involved from case to case. Structural differences between or within the individual countries in fact call for differing, objective-oriented measures. It should therefore be left to the individual countries to decide on their own, within a certain framework, on the measures necessary to bring about structural improvements.

In this connection, the rules of Article 92 et seq. of the EEC Treaty need to be observed which lay down the obligation to inform the Commission on, and obtain its approval for, all such aids of whatever nature which are granted by a State or through State resources and which favour only certain undertakings or only the production of certain goods. This, however, applies only if such aids are apt to restrict competition between Member States.

If the provisions of the EEC Treaty are applied consistently, there will be no threat of sectoral distortions of competition resulting from discriminating privileges.

V. Summary

The realization of an integrated economic area embracing all EC Member States depends on conditions being created that are similar to those prevailing in a national domestic market, which means that competition between business enterprises should not be distorted by national legislation. In times of economic crises, the differences in tax burdens like other factors affecting competition - viz. primarily

personnel costs and the development of the national currency's external value - tend to grow in importance. These differences in tax burdens are characterized by the size of the percentage rate of tax revenue to GNP, by differences in the structures of tax systems and by differing methods of determining profits for tax purposes.
A first step towards the harmonization of direct taxes might be a standardization of the rules governing the determination of profits for tax purposes. This could be based on the Fourth EC Directive on the harmonization of the provisions of commercial law relating to annual accounts. It should also be authoritative within the EC for matters connected with the determining of profits for tax purposes.

The problem of tax law resulting from such authoritativeness would have to be solved by means of a renewed attempt to reach agreement.

Now that the Fourth EC Directive has brought about a material step forward towards harmonization of commercial law, further efforts should be made to continue harmonization of tax law on the basis of that directive. In this connection one can but hope that the efforts to align tax law will not have the same fate as the Council Directive on a common tax system for parent and subsidiary companies (Group Directive), the Council Directive on a common tax system for mergers and split-ups of, and contributions of assets to, companies in different Member States (Merger Directive) , both of which have been pending adoption for ten years, and the Proposal for a Council Regulation on the European Cooperation Grouping which for four years has come no nearer to its realization.

Annex, Table 1

Comparison of "combined taxation and social security ratios" [1)] in the EC - 1977 -

States	Taxation ratio	Social security ratio	Combined taxation and social security ratio
Belgium	28.5	12.5	41.0
Denmark	43.8	0.7	44.5
Federal Republic of Germany	25.1	14.1	39.2
France	24.9	15.4	40.3
Great Britain	28.7	6.8	35.5
Ireland	29.7	4.5	34.2
Italy	21.3	13.8	35.1
Luxembourg	35.4	17.2	52.6
Netherlands	29.3	18.1	47.4

1) Sum of taxation ratio and social security ratio in relationship to GNP.

Source: German Federal Ministry of Finance: Finanzbericht 1979

Annex, Table 2

Tax receipts by categories of tax within the EC [1] in terms of percentages of overall tax revenue

Category of tax	Belgium 1976	Fed.Rep.of Germany 1977	Denmark 1976	France 1976	Great Britain 1976	Italy 1976	Luxembourg 1976	Netherlands 1977
Taxes on income and property								
1. Income tax	46.3	42.2	55.7	18.3	47.0	23.9	36.2	43.3
2. Corporation tax	11.1	5.6	3.6	10.6	6.4	5.6	17.7	11.2
3. Capital yields tax	-	1.1	0.2	-	-	13.9	1.0	1.0
4. Property tax	-	2.1	0.4	-	-	-	1.2	0.7
5. Other tax on income and property [2]	-	10.7 [3]	3.3	13.1	12.6 [4]	-	12.3	0.1
Total direct Taxes	57.9	61.9	63.2	42.0	66.0	43.4	68.4	56.3
Taxes on consumption								
1. VAT	27.2	20.9	17.4	43.1	11.0	24.6	16.4	28.6
2. Other excises and taxes on consumption	1[illegible].2	15.0	17.2	9.5	19.4	26.3 [5]	11.8	10.3
Total indirect Taxes	33.4	35.9	34.6	52.6	30.4	50.9	28.2	38.9

1) Not including Ireland for which no recent figures are available.
2) Especially land, buildings and trade taxes.
3) Of which 8.9 % are trade taxes.
4) Taxes on land and buildings only.
5) Of which 12.9 % are hydrocarbon oil taxes.

Source: German Federal Ministry of Finance

Annex, Table 3

Scales of income tax in the EC[1)]

States[2)]	Rate system (SE=segment of income FR=flat rate F=formula)	Rates of scale in percentage terms[3)] from - to	Income tax scales 1978[4)]					
			Starting rate of scale			Marginal rate of scale		
			Percent	For segments of income up to ...		Percent	For segments of income of ... and more	
				In national currency	In DM[5)]		In national currency	In DM[5)]
1	2	3	4	5	6	7	8	9
Belgium	20 SE	17 - 72	17	bfr 94,000	6,054	76.32[6)]	bfr 4 m.	257,000
Fed.Rep. of Germany	F	22 - 56	22	DM 16,019	16,019	56	DM 130,020	130,020
Denmark -Nat.govt. -Municipalities	3 SE FR	16 - 44 22[7)]	36,4[8)]	dkr 71,800	26,315	61,6[9)]	dkr 127,800	46,839
France	12 SE	5 - 60	5	FF 7,600	3,405	60	FF 119,100	53,357
Great Britain	10 SE	34 - 83[10)]	34	Ƀ 6,000	24,540	83	Ƀ 21,000	85,890
Ireland	6 SE	20 - 60	20	Ƀ 500	2,045	60	Ƀ 7.000	28,630
Italy -Nat.govt. -Political sub-divisions	32 SE FR	10 - 72 15[11)]	23,5	L 3 m.	7,260	76,2	L 550 m.	1,331,000
Luxembourg	18 SE	18 - 57	18	lfr 95,400	6,144	57	lfr 919,800	59,235
Netherlands	10 SE	20 - 72	20	hfl 6,164	5,745	72	hfl 166,945	155,593

Annex, Table 3

1) Basis rate scales for persons without dependants whenever there are differentiated scales of rates.
2) Where in addition to the national government political sub-divisions also impose general income taxes, the latter are included in the figures.
3) Nominal rates (with no regard to multipliers, scale adjustments or the like).
4) Including multipliers, scale adjustments or the like; combination of national government taxes with those of political sub-divisions if applicable.
5) Converted into DM at rates of exchange prevailing in January 1978.
6) 72 % national government tax, plus 6 % of the amount of that tax as a municipal surcharge; ceiling of overall tax is 71.55 % (67.5 % national tax plus 6 % of the amount of that tax as a municipal surcharge).
7) Average rate 1977.
8) 14.4 % national government tax, 22 % municipal surcharge.
9) 39.6 % national government tax, 22 % municipal surcharge, ceiling for overall tax.
10) For earned income; for investment income over Ŀ 1,500 an additional 10 % (up to Ŀ 2,000) or 15 % (income segments over Ŀ 2,000). In the 1978 budget speech the following tax rates were proposed for capital gains: Ŀ 0 - 1,000: 0 %; Ŀ 1,000 - 5,000: 15 %; Ŀ 5,000 - 9,500: graduated upwards to 30 %; over Ŀ 9,500: 30 %.
11) Not on income from employment and from capital yields; deductible from base of national government tax.

Source: German Federal Ministry of Finance; International Bureau of Fiscal Documentation.

Annex, Table 4

Corporation tax systems in the EC - 1978

Corporation tax systems	States	Tax rates [1]
Uniform taxation of total profits	Luxembourg Netherlands	20 % to 40 % [2] 46 % [3]
Credit given for part of corporation tax attributable to distributed profits	Belgium	33 - 48 % [4]; 57,5 % of distributed profits allowed as a credit against income tax.
	Denmark	37 %; 15 % of distributed profits allowed as credit against income tax.
	France	50 %; 50 % of distributed profits allowed as credit against income tax.
	Great Britain	52 % [5]; 34/66 of distributed profits allowed as credit against income tax.
	Ireland	45 % [6]; 35/65 of distributed profits allowed as credit against income tax. Companies who make a 3 % increase in the number of their employees in one year, the corporation tax rate is in future to be no more than 25 %.
System of crediting in full of corporation taxes attributable to distributed profits	Italy	36,25 % on total profits [7]; credit allowed for 1/3 of dividend.
System of "split" tax rate, full credit allowed for corporation tax attributable to distributed profits	Fed. Rep. of Germany	56 % 36 % on distributed profits; full crediting of tax on distributed profits against income tax.

1) Including taxes, if any, of political sub-divisions; account was taken of deductibility, if any, of the latter taxes from national government tax.
2) Scale of rates progressing evenly in a straight line; maximum rate applied to incomes over lfr 1.312 m.
3) Reduced starting rate of 45 % on profits up to hfl 50,000.
4) Scale of rates progressing evenly in a straight line; maximum rate of 48 % on income over bfr 15 m.
5) 42 % on profits up to £ 40,000; for profits up to £ 65,000 this rate rises progressively to 52 %. Proposed change: 42 % up to £ 65,000; progressive increase up to 52 %, the latter to be charged on profits of £ 85,000.
6) 35 % on profits up to £ 25,000; for profits up to £ 35,000 this rate rises progressively up to 45 % as from April 1978.
7) 25 % national government tax, 15 % political sub-division tax (deductible from base of national government tax).

<u>Sources:</u> German Federal Ministry of Finance; International Bureau of Fiscal Documentation.

Annex, Table 5

Depreciation for tax purposes in the EC - 1978

States	Buildings		
	Straight line depreciation rate	Depreciation period, years	Total depreciation period, years
1	2	3	4
1. Belgium	3[1)] 5[2)]	- -	33 20
2. Fed. Rep. of Germany	a) 2[4)] b) 3,5 2,0 1,0	 12 20 18	50 50
3. Denmark	6[6)] 2	10 20	30
4. France	5[8)] 2 bis 5	-	20
5. Great Britain	50+4[10)] 4 2	1 11 1	13
6. Ireland	50+4[10)] 4 2	1 11 1	13
7. Italy[11)]	3+15 3 1	3 15 1	19
8. Luxembourg	2[1)] 3 1	 33 1	50 34
9. Netherlands	a) 1,5[13)] 1 b) 3 1	66 1 33 1	67 34

Annex, Table 5

Depreciation for tax purposes in the EC - 1978

States	Movable fixed assets			
	Straight line depreciation rate	Depreciation period, years	Total depreciation period, years	declining balance method
1	5	6	7	8
1. Belgium	a) 10 b) 33 1/3	-	10 3	yes[3)] no
2. Fed. Rep. of Germany	10	-	10	no[5)]
3. Denmark	-	-	-	yes, 30%[7)]
4. France	10 bis 25		10 bis 4	yes[9)]
5. Great Britain	Initial rate of depreciation optional, i.e. anything up to 100 %. The residual value is written off by application of the declining balance method.			yes, 25%[7)]
6. Ireland	Optional annual rates of depreciation up to a			
7. Italy[11)]	a) 10+15 10 5 b) 12,5+15 5	3 2 1 3 1	6 5	no no
8. Luxembourg	8 4	12 1	13	yes[12)]
9. Netherlands	10	-	10	yes[14)]

Annex, Table 5

1) Office buildings.
2) Industrial buildings.
3) Since 1977: Declining balance depreciation for all fixed asset items, the maximum rate being equal to double the line rate; the ceiling of 20 % of the book value has been abolished (genuine double-rate depreciation).
4) For buildings completed before 1 January 1925: 2,5 % of purchase price or production cost.
5) The declining balance rates are equal to two and one half times the straight line rates or 25 % of the book value, whichever is the lower.
6) Not for office buildings or company housing; certain buildings (e.g. hotels, garages, laboratories and storage buildings) may be depreciated at a rate of 4 % during the first 10 years they are in use and at a rate of 1 % during the following years.
7) Pooled declining balance method.
8) Declining balance depreciation of buildings and hotels of a used for a period not exceeding 15 years.
9) For periods of use of 3 to 4 years one and one half times the straight line rates, for periods of 5 to 6 years double the straight line rates, and for periods of more than 6 years two and one half times the straight line rates.
10) Allowed for industrial buildings only. Ireland is planning to introduce free depreciation of up to 100 % during the first year.
11) Depreciation of an asset is based on its book value, increased through multiplication by a revaluation factor of 1.4 if acquired or produced before 1972, by 1.3 % if acquired or produced during 1972 and by 1.2 if acquired or produced during 1973.
12) Double the straight line rate but not more than 20 % of the book value.

Annex, Table 5

13) For buildings constructed outside congested areas, accelerated depreciation may additionally be taken in the first years at an annual rate of 25 % of production cost.

14) Declining balance method must be applied in accordance with generally accepted accounting principles; normally, the rate is double the straight line rate.

Sources: German Federal Ministry of Finance: Finanzrundschau 1978 p. 83; Commission of the European Communities; Internationale Wirtschaftsbriefe No. 21/1977.

Annex, Table 6

General tax benefits offered in regard to expenditure on capital investments in the EC - 1978 -

(Example: Machinery with a useful life of 10 years)

States	Maximum rate of depreciation for wear and tear and in other forms [1], allowed for tax purposes, in terms of percentage of purchase price or replacement cost			
	during first year	after 3 years	after 7 years	after 10 years
1	2	3	4	5
1. Belgium	20	48,8	89.1	100
2. Fed. Rep. of Germany	25	57.8	86.7	100
3. Denmark	30	65.7	91.8	100
4. France	30	65.7	91.8	100
5. Great Britain	100 [2] 25 [3]	100.0 57.8	100.0 86.7	100 100
6. Ireland	100	100.0	100.0	100
7. Italy	25	75.0	89.4	100
8. Luxembourg	20	48.8	80.4	100
9. Netherlands	20	48.8	80.4	100

1) Including general accelerated depreciation, investment allowances and deductions from tax payable, other than those restricted to specific periods of time.

2) Special arrangement since 1972.

3) General statutory rule.

Source: German Federal Ministry of Finance.

Discussion

Mr. Ole Bus Henriksen, General Director
(EC-Commission)

We have this morning had two interesting contributions on how to arrange our moves towards harmonization of corporation tax in Europe. It is natural for me as director-general in the services of the Commission to try to bridge the two different approaches which have been presented to us in these contributions. We heard Commissioner Burke, this morning, put emphasis on speedy action in the field of harmonization of tax systems. And we hear Prof. Vogel in his extremely interesting contribution just now say that he differs to some extent in this attitude, that he would rather see that we put emphasis right away on the harmonization of the tax base. My attempt at bridging the two contributions consists especially in saying that, for the Commission, the problem of harmonization of the tax base is of course a problem of high priority and the way in which Commissioner Burke presented our policy this morning must not in anyway be taken to imply that we do not want to see rapid movement in the field of harmonization of tax bases.

Indeed, we are in the process of attacking this problem. Prof. Vogel is certainly right in pointing out that the fact that in a couple of years we shall have the 4th company directive means that we will have to regard this problem with an even higher urgency than hitherto since we will want to see a close link between the profit-and-loss-accounts of firms. We will want of course a situation where firms can rely on the same data base for both purposes; we will not want the Community to impose new administrative burdens on firms for the sake of the regulations found in the various company law and fiscal regulations. I cannot, and already for reasons of time, go into much detail on this. We tend to move towards the assessment that it is necessary to draw a distinguishing line between what you could call the normal scheme of corporation tax on one side and the whole field of special incentives for sectoral or regional purposes on the other side - a distinction which Prof. Vogel also evidently was fully aware of the need to draw. We believe that we will have to try to hammer out a set of what you could call normal regulations. And in doing so we certainly have to keep a close eye on what has already happened in the 4th company directive. I am not saying that we shall systematically use the 4th company directive as the guide in this work, but certainly we feel the need, as implied in what I have said already, for complete consistency between the new action in the fiscal field and the action already taken in the company law field.

It is obvious that we do not solve all the mince of problems by trying to define what should be the normal corporation tax scheme. It is in a way just a manner of redefining the problem. We will still face the underlining problems - which Prof. Vogel also stressed - of evaluation of assets and of depreciation.

And in our further work in this field we find it to be an enormous benefit for the Commission services to have the close co-operations not only with the national authorities but also to be able to draw on the expertise gathered in this Conféderation and we are looking forward to future occasions to discuss these technical problems and to hear your points of view. We certainly are grateful for the occasion we have for the

Commission services to attend at this conference which is a necessary input for us in our future work.

Mr. Karl Krammig, Steuerberater (Germany)

During the overall view given by Commissioner Burke this morning on the efforts made towards a harmonizing of taxes within the European Communities, I missed one tax. Perhaps because this particular tax flows already entirely into the funds of the European Communities and for this reason the interest in a further harmonization - may I add jokingly - may have disappeared. He spoke of turnover tax and of the other consumer taxes and of direct taxes but nothing was said of excise duties. Taxes on goods imported from third countries have already been harmonized to a great extent by the Community tarifs. The regulations concerning the levying of custom taxes have also been harmonized. But something is still missing and this is what I wanted to ask Mr. Burke: when can we expect a harmonization of the conditions which lead to a payment of customs duties because, in fact the different custom duty conditions within the EEC create a gap in the harmonization of custom taxes and can incite dishonest people to turn third country goods into Community goods in a dishonest way, which in another Community country will be recognized as third country and the latter - if you will pardon the expression - are left sitting pretty. If this is to be prevented, then the conditions which lead to a payment of custom duties should be harmonized as quickly as possible within the EC.

Mr. Ole Bus'Henriksen, General Director
(EC-Commission)

I will try to answer in much the same way as this is not a problem of fiscal harmonization. It's a problem of customs administration, and for one thing, we don't deal with that in Mr. Burke's department. But for another thing, and that is the substance of the answer, the Commission is fully aware of the customs administrative problems which from time to time hit the headlines of the European press. And there is a major effort going on to try to fuse the various loop-holes which invariably exist in a complicated administrative system as is the levying of customs in a union consisting of 9 member states which have started out in quite different positions. This is not a problem which is not being handled in the Commission.

NN

It would seem necessary to explain the disent which exists between the views held by Mr. Burke and Prof. Vogel. While the Commission, with regard to its efforts towards greater harmonization, attaches more importance to the last stages of tax levy, namely to the question of regulations concerning imputation for cooperation tax, Prof. Vogel, tends on the other hand, to place it toward the beginning, with a harmonization of the tax base. I would like to know why the Commission does not take advantage of the progress made - with regard to the harmonization of the tax base in the 4th directive concerning provisions for evaluation in the commercial balance - to intensify its work in this field, instead of concentrating on the harmonization of cooperation taxes, where not very much has been done so far.

Prof. Dr. Horst Vogel, Steuerberater and Rechtsanwalt (Germany)

We are now forced to take a decision - I do not know if this was sufficiently stressed in my paper - because we must put a common system of commercial law into application in two years. For this reason the national legislators must say to what extent the harmonized regulations for commercial law in Europe also apply to taxation matters. This is why the Commission should start thinking now as to how harmonization could be brought about, also in the field of taxation. When shall we ever be given a better opportunity to reconcile commercial law and tax law, now that the procedure is underway with the EC directive. I would like to give this a higher priority than the question of the harmonization of the systems of cooperation taxes, where strong philosophies of different tendencies find their application.

Mr. Ole Bus Henriksen, General Director (EC-Commission)

I think it's difficult and probably not even relevant to distinguish between what could be regarded as the first chain in the process of living, tax and corporation and what should be regarded as the subsequent elements in this chain.

Certainly all of these elements in a given country go into one unity and it is the composite result of these factors which have an influence on the competitive situation of producers in member States. Prof. Vogel speaks of the situation now where we are compelled to take decision. I would add to that, we are compelled to take a decision in the field of the harmonization of the tax base. We cannot let this problem rest, we don't want to let it rest, we want to attack it, we are attacking it. But we are compelled to take a decision also in the field of harmonisation of tax-systems; for a number of years already, but nothing has happened, as Commissioner Burke explained, the problem is still pending before the European Parliament. Once it is through the European Parliament, it will be before the Council, and that will take some time as we all know. And the lack of harmonisation of tax systems has a very strong distortive effect on capital flows in the community, as Mr. Burke made a point of this morning. I shall not repeat the arguments. The conclusion seen from my point of view is, that it is actually compellingly necessary to move on both scores. I don't like to regard this as a theoretical problem whether you ought to attack one problem, for theoretical or hypothetical or academic reasons, before the other.

But we have a real and a political situation in the Community where we have a fargoing and we think constructive proposal in front of one of the institutions of the Community already. The sooner we can get that through the better, because the sooner we will be able to attack the specific distortions due to differences in tax-systems. And we are with you for the necessity to go along as quickly as it is at all possible with the effort, the supplementary effort, the likewise unavoidable effort of harmonizing the tax-base.

The Taxation of Companies in Europe, with Special Consideration of the Effects of Double Taxation Agreements

Desmond Airey
Chartered Accountant, former President of the Institute of Taxation, London

The subject matter laid before the assembly was the taxation of companies in Europe, with special consideration of the effects of double taxation agreements. Commissioner Burke, in his morning paper "The harmonisation of taxation in Europe", had already given an outline of the need for harmonisation and the stages by which it could possibly be achieved. In the course of the present address (in the afternoon) it was not possible to give a review in depth of the tax systems of each constituent country let alone the double taxation implications in respect of companies, their shareholders or loan creditors whose rewards are subject to withholding tax.

Fortunately, in practice, it is not necessary for any one person to have at his fingertips the detailed working knowledge of all the relevant tax systems. At the present time it is possible to obtain good local advice from competent practitioners who have an up-to-date knowledge of the practice and pitfalls prevailing at the time, in respect of one given country. There appears to be no real substitute for the advice given by local practitioners in respect of local (i. e. national) taxation affairs.

One of the side issues, at this point, is the liberalisation of the profession of taxation practitioners between countries, at least within the Common Market, which could possibly lead to more effective taxation practice. In the course of this paper, however, there was not the wish to dwell, at length, on this particular point.

Constitutional Matters.

Fortunately, in Europe, on this side of the Iron Curtain, there is at least one point in common regarding the introduction of taxation laws. In each country they are brought about by a legislative body. The task of raising and administering such taxes is then in the hands of the executive authority and finally, such administration, is under the review of the courts. Inevitably, the degree of overlap between the legislative body, the executive and the courts varies from country to country according to their relevant constitutional laws.

There is a wide difference between countries in the matter of timing legislation. In the United Kingdom tax is raised by the central government as an annual tax. Such taxes are raised on a temporary basis from year to year. Each and every year Parliament has to give its consent to such taxes and the absence of such consent vitiates the powers to collect taxes. The only practical point which needs to be raised at this stage is that, at present within Europe and certainly not within the Common Market, there is not any uniform process for introducing taxation legislation, which not only changes the rate of tax but other fundamental rules relating to the yardstick of measurement of such tax, the assessment thereof and the collection. This means, in turn, that if one refers to one taxation system with certainty in one country, inevitably the other country concerned is going through a stage of changing law. This has particular practical reference to dealing with the practical application of double taxation agreements between countries.

This aspect, in itself, would not be too bad but for the fact that in the United Kingdom for example, there is a growing tendancy to legislate by pronouncement followed, at a later date, by due legislation. It is hoped that if there is to be any form of harmonisation in the future, this means of legislation by pronouncement will cease, except in matters concerning the most blatant of tax avoidance schemes.

To summarize constitutional matters, it is as well, in dealing with the taxation affairs of another country, to have at least a brief understanding of the legislative means by which tax laws are introduced, the executive means by which they are administered and the means under which they can be reviewed by appeal procedure or a negotiated settlement.

Companies

In order to understand the taxation system in any country, relating to companies, it is necessary to have at least an outline in the following aspects:

a. The various types of companies (corporations). Most countries have at least two types of companies namely the Public company and the smaller Private company. In some cases, quasi partnerships are treated as companies. In other cases such partnerships are treated on an individual basis i. e. each individual partner is treated as a separate entity. For example, in the United Kingdom there are two simple divisions, namely the Public company and the Private company. These divisions are of paramount importance for company law purposes but of no great importance for tax purposes. The United Corporation Tax is raised on all companies, large and small, under the same coded law. Partnerships are not, in any way, treated as companies except where the member of the partnership is itself a company. Even then the tax treatment as a company is confined to that corporate partner member.

This structure may be contrasted with the French system whereby the Sociétés Anonymes, Sociétés à Responsabilité Limitée and Sociétés en Commandite par Actions are brought into the net of company taxation.

Likewise in Belgium, we have a variety of entities which can have corporate status.

It is, therefore, necessary in the case of each country to understand the concept of what is a company (as opposed to an individual entity) chargeable to tax.

b. The definition of directors, control and management. Here again there is a divergence between countries in the matter of law regarding the definitions of directors, of control and of management. Furthermore, the importance of such definitions and such status varies between countries.

c. The concept of income, the divisions and types of such income and the measurement of such income. Perhaps in this respect the United Kingdom taxes are far more complex than elsewhere in Europe. In this country not only is there a division between types of income, there is also a serious diversion in the method of measurement of such income and the treatment of losses in each category of income.

At page 3 of Appendix I it may be seen that in respect of the income of a United Kingdom company there are several types of income (apart from the concept of chargeable gains on disposal of capital items). Each type of income has its own rules regarding measurement of income, treatment of losses and the amount to be brought into charge for taxation purposes as well as having different rules regarding allowance of expenses and deemed the date of receipt of income in the case of each category.

These rules, apart from being unnecessarily complex, cause serious difficulty of alignment of taxes in dealing with double taxation agreements. Furthermore, in the United Kingdom, there is a special tax on certain profits on land (whether realised or not) known as Development Land Tax. This tax is chargeable upon individuals and companies (irrespective of other taxes) having a top rate of 80 %, no allowance for losses and no counterpart for double taxation purposes.

In the case of the United Kingdom all distributions to shareholders in the lifetime of a company i. e. before liquidation has commenced are treated as dividends. There is no such concept - since 1965 - of a capital distribution to shareholders. This aspect is not uniformly accepted in other countries.

The purpose of this paper so far has been to identify the need to understand the constitutional concepts under which taxes arise and then to understand the constitution of the companies who as taxpayers bear the incidence of such tax.

It is now necessary to examine the types of taxes:

Taxes on Companies

a. The nature of the tax and the mechanics of its implementation. It is necessary, in the case of the tax system of each country (with particular reference to taxes on companies), to understand the nature of the tax itself. It is, also, necessary to understand the mechanics of its implementation. That is to say, firstly, is the company within the ambit of the tax. Secondly, does the tax cover income alone. Thirdly, does it cover income and capital or is there no distinction between these two items.

In the same context, it is necessary to understand how far geographically each country extends the right to tax companies. For example, in France there is the territorial concept of taxation, in the United Kingdom there is the world wide concept of taxation and in the United States, with particular reference to the state of California, there is a divergence of views between the Federal Government and the Californian State's Government as to the extent to which state taxes may be raised in and out of the United States. Here again, the divergences are between territorial tax and world wide tax.

Turning to matters of trading income, it is then necessary to understand the concept of inventories and the measurement of such inventories for taxation purposes. In itself, the inventory is a comparatively small item concerning tax legislation but in practical effect the concept of measurement of inventories has a great influence on the measure of trading profit, particularly taking into account the increase in value due to inflation and the decrease in value due to erosion of time and obsolescence.

The particular rules for each country must be thoroughly understood. Each country has its own way of dealing with inventory values and with inventory inflation and obsolescence.

b. Inflation index. Each country has its own method of dealing with inflation so far as taxation is concerned. The simplest tax systems in this respect are where inflation is ignored, but simplicity and fair taxation do not often go hand in hand.

c. The next factor which has to be borne in mind is the

matter of accountancy procedures and conventions under which accounts are drawn up to show profit and to show assets and liabilities in a balance sheet form.

At the time of writing this paper the directives on company law relevant to corporate accounting and taxation were as follows:

First directive	Approved 1968 Substance - dealing with the ultra-vires rules
Second directive	Approved 1966 Substance - separation of private and public companies, minimum capital and limitation on distribution and interim dividends
Third directive	Drafts dated 1970, 1973 and 1975 - not yet approved concerning mergers
Fourth directive	Drafts dated 1971, 1974 and 1977 Approved 1978 Substance - the format and rules of accounting
Fifth directive	Draft dated 1972 - not yet approved Substance - the structure, management and audit of companies
Sixth directive	Drafts dated 1972 and 1975 - not yet approved Substance - prospectuses

Seventh directive	Draft dated 1976 - not yet approved Substance - consolidated accounts
Eighth directive	Draft dated 1978 - not yet approved Substance - qualification and duties of auditors

It may be seen that until further progress is made in these accounting matters the prospect of harmonisation or at least reconciliation of taxation concepts remain only as a future ideal.

d. Capital expenditure. In this respect the methods of granting the allowances against profits for depreciation vary considerably. The timing of the tax relief, ranging from giving 100 % immediately, through a scale of depreciation charges, to giving no relief whatsoever, is a very difficult problem when considering double taxation relief.

A further aspect in this matter is the clawback of such relief upon the disposal of the relevant asset which qualifies for relief in the first instance.

e. The effect of subsidies. There is no uniform practice between countries in the matter of treatment of central government, local government and private subsidies, both in respect of income and capital. This can substantially affect the yardstick of measurement of income with particular reference to long term contracts as in the construction industry.

Further difficulty is that the purpose of subsidies range from supporting trades and industries which would otherwise be uneconomical to enticing investment lucrative or desirable form of trade or industry.

f. The concept of losses both for capital and for income vary from country to country and in each case the consequences of the methods of relief must be thoroughly understood.

g. Withholding taxes. These can occur on expenditure payments, on interest and royalty payments and on dividends. The nature of these withholding taxes must be examined in detail.

EEC Directives

At this stage we are dealing with draft ideals which do not have effect on current tax computations. However, it is necessary to consider the directives when coming to future planning on large scale investment and large scale transfers of income. In this respect, the concept of groups of companies (with particular reference to international groups of companies) and the concept of branches as opposed to separate companies must be examined and understood in the case of the tax system for each country.

One of the difficulties which arises regarding future planning is, that, as more detailed disciplines come into operation, an increasing number of corporate structures, particularly the smaller companies which form the greater part of corporate bodies in all countries, will be inevitably excluded from the full effect of such disciplines. However, in terms of dealing with double taxation agreements, they will not be so excluded. We have, therefore, a situation in planning for the future where inconsistencies in measurement of income and capital will continue to exist for possibly decades hence in respect of the smaller entities which account for a large part of income and capital investment and will, therefore, continue to give rise to difficulties in applying double taxation agreements in circumstances where the taxation laws of two countries to an agreement are based on entirely different concepts.

The paper, at this stage, has been designed by way of an attempt to analyse the areas which need to be examined in order to arrive at an understanding of the income of capital gains which, in the hands of a company, can be subject to double taxation.

To summarise, at this stage, there has been examined the constitutional authority for raising taxes, the nature of the taxing body which make such tax demands and the concept of a company which bears incidence of such tax followed by the concept of capital and income within the company. The vital stage comes at the point of time when there is need to consider distribution of such capital or profits. For this purpose, it is necessary to look internally within the bounds of the European Economic Community, then outwardly, but still within the bounds of the European continent, that is to say, dealing between EEC countries and countries such as Switzerland, Spain and Scandinavia and then looking geographically further abroad to the problems which arise in dealing with the United States, the Middle East, Japan and Australia.

It is in this area where harmonisation of accounting concepts and of taxation within the EEC will still leave double taxation problems in dealing with these external countries. The original OEDC draft which has formed an excellent basis for double taxation agreements can still only deal with fundamental aspects of law and not variation of concepts of identification of income, capital, taxpayers and constitutions.

<u>Double Taxation</u>

The areas to consider are:

i) Taxation of overseas branches' profits
ii) Withholding taxes on income payments
iii) Withholding taxes on dividends and deemed distributions

It is in the context of these three aspects that we draw together the threads of the pattern set out in this paper.

The first concept to question is whether to have an overseas branch or an overseas subsidiary of an existing corporate body. At this stage, it is necessary to look at the relevant double taxation treaty. Tax in a country does not normally arise for a branch unless there is a permanent establishment in the same country. If a permanent establishment arises, then it is generally more favourable to have a subsidiary unless the branch profits are not taxed until repatriated.

The practical difficulty then arises in comparing the measurement of profit for tax purposes in the country of origin and the country of repatriation of profits. It is in this respect that the timing of relief for depreciation and for inflation may differ considerably. If losses are foreseen, the branch situation can generally be of greater advantage than the subsidiary company.

An extension of this concept is the use of a low tax base country into which to repatriate the branch or subsidiary company profits. This procedure is subject to anti-avoidance legislation of which Article 14 (France 1974) is but an example. Likewise, in the double taxation agreement between the United Kingdom and Switzerland various anti-avoidance provisions have been inserted.

A cynical view of some double taxation agreements is that they are designed for anti-avoidance purposes rather than for relief purposes.

The next area of consideration relates to royalties and lump sum payments for knowhow. In each case, it is necessary to look to the particular double taxation agreement to avoid the pitfall of the recipient being unnecessarily taxed and the payer being deprived of tax relief on the payment or on both. Lump sum payments present particular difficulty as payments which give rise to commercial protection, such as patents, can be treated differently to 'knowhow'. Often the commercial advantages and the tax advantages are in conflict.

It is, therefore, necessary in considering such payments to design the routing thereof to avoid unnecessary incidence of taxation. Thus a payment from country A to country B is sometimes routed through country C and country D to avoid or lessen the incidence of withholding tax.

Similar consideration has to be given to the structuring of interest payments.

In the case of royalties and interest, the structuring problem is threefold by reference to Tax treaties:

a) to avoid withholding tax where possible
b) to avoid the charge to tax on the recipient
c) to avoid disallowance of tax relief in the hands of the recipient

There now has to be considered the niceties of tax on distributions. If there were no such factors as distributions there would not be the need to consider the following fundamental differences in the tax systems. The three main tax systems within the EEC are:

a) The classical system which draws little distinction between distributed and undistributed profits.

b) The Imputation System. This levies tax uniformly on distributed and undistributed income, but gives a credit to the recipient of the distributed income.

c) The split rate system. This system taxes distributed profits at a lower rate than undistributed profits.

There are set out in appendices I and II comparatively simple examples of the operation of a branch and a subsidiary company pertaining to a United Kingdom business. Even in these examples some unpleasant pitfalls occur which preclude in part, double taxation relief.

It is now necessary to refer back to appendix I. The purpose of this appendix is to analyse the various taxation concepts in detail and under sub-titles. This enables such concepts to be compared and contrasted from country to country. It would be ideal to have such an appendix prepared for each country and in practice it is necessary to do so. Lack of space prevents such a series of appendices being attached hereto.

Appendix III is designed to illustrate the basic differences in computation between the classical, the imputation and the split rate systems which, at present, prevail.

It is hoped that this pattern of analysis of concepts will indicate the large amount of work which is still needed to be done in order to reconcile, if not harmonise, taxation systems so that in practice, double taxation relief agreements will operate without the need, on the taxpayer's part, to resort to artificialities or avoidance measures.

APPENDIX I

Country United Kingdom

1. Basis of Taxation Law

Annually by consent of Parliament and subject to Parliamentary legislation.

2. Legislative Authority

Method of introduction of legislation and annual date:

a) March/April. The Chancellor of the Exchequer announces the terms of his Budget. The Bill is presented to Parliament.

b) April/July. The relevant House of Commons committee discusses and amends the Bill.

c) July/August. The Bill receives Royal Assent and becomes effective as an Act of Parliament. The dates upon which various items in the Act become effective are stated in the Act itself.

3. Executive Authority	Assessment	Collection
i) Centrally	Board of Inland Revenue	
ii) Locally	Tax Inspectors	Tax Collectors

(These are separated branches of the Inland Revenue. They act in unison .

4. Judical Authority

i) Ministerial	The Lord Chancellor	
ii) Courts	a)	General or Special Commissioners (largely by choice of the taxpayer)
	b)	High Court
	c)	Court of Appeal (This stage can be by-passed in certain instances)
	d)	House of Lords

5. Method of Variation

Rates	Annually - Finance Act
Procedures	Basically, by means of the Finance Act. However, the Board of Inland Revenue have wide administrative powers which generally are not abused.
Other Matters	Concessions: The Board have substantial powers to grant concessions, the majority of which are published and are available to all taxpayers.

6. International Powers

Double Taxation Agreements	The Board of Inland Revenue, in conjunction with other Ministries have wide powers to negotiate agreements. These agreements have to be ratified by Parliament, after signature.

7. Types of Corporation

a) Public - (Quoted
(Unquoted

b) Private - forbidden to be quoted

For corporation tax purposes there are only two categories

a) Close companies i.e. controlled by a defined number of shareholders, loan holders or directors.

b) Non-Close companies

8. Concept of Directors

Any person who is able to exercise the powers or who assumes (by conduct) the powers of a director, irrespective of whether or not he is so appointed.

9. Concept of Shareholders

a) Any person registered as a shareholder

b) In certain cases, relating to close companies, any person who can exercise the powers of a shareholder.

10. Concept of Income (for corporations)

Chargeable to Corporation Tax	(	Trading Income
	(	Rental Income
	(	Interest Receivable
	(	Royalties Receivable
	(	Deemed income from anti-avoidance charges
	(	Overseas Income (e.g. foreign dividends, interest and royalties)
	(	Building Society Interest (grossed up)
Not chargeable to Corporation Tax	-	U.K. Dividends

11. Mearurement of Income

Each category has its own rules of measuring receipts and expenses - losses etc. Only trading losses can be set against all other types of income. (see paragraph 23(b) below)

12. Concept of Capital (Assets)

The concept of capital for accounting purposes is clearly identifiable. However, for corporation tax purposes, capital is simply the residue which is not treated as income receipts or income expenditure.

13. Measurement of Capital

This concept comes into use in measuring the cost of the asset which is allowable for capital allowances (depreciation) purposes. Here again, the accountancy concept can differ widely from the concepts laid down in the taxing statutes. The same pitfall arises in measuring capital gains.

14. Types of Taxes on Income and Gains

There is one uniform tax (known as corporation tax) chargeable on the total of all income and capital gains after deducting allowable charges for the year and trading losses brought forward from prior periods. The rate is 52% subject relief where the profits (i.e. income plus capital gains) does not exceed £85,000.

15. Other taxes on Income Payments

Withholding tax on

a) patent royalties
b) mining royalties
c) interest payments
d) rents payable to overseas persons
e) certain land transaction payments (this is an anti-avoidance measure)

16. Taxes on distribution of

Income: There is no withholding tax. Advance corporation tax is payable by the company equal to 33/67ths of the cash distribution. This advance corporation tax (ACT) can be set against subsequent liabilities to pay corporation tax (subject to a specific restriction) where the dividend exceeds the relevant chargeable income. The set off is also restricted to the income element of the corporation tax assessment i.e. although the income and gains are assessed to corporation tax in one total figure. The ACT relief is restricted to the income element of the assessment.

Capital: Capital distributions are treated as dividends except in liquidation.

17. Effect of Liquidation

a) Distributions are capital receipts and are not treated as dividends.

b) In the case of controlled companies (Close companies) the relevant income for specific periods is deemed to have been distributed as dividends.

18. Effect of Subsidies

Local / National: Contributions towards revenue expenditure are treated as a deduction from such expenditure or as trading income e.g. agricultural prices subsidies are treated as chargeable income.

Contributions towards capital are treated as a deduction for the relevant outlay.

19. Capital Expenditure

Method of Amortization - Methods used for accountancy purposes differ in rate and timing from tax reliefs for depreciation. There are difference scales for:

Plant and Machinery
Industrial Buildings
Agricultural Buildings

19. Capital Expenditure (cont'd)

Mines and oil wells
Shipping
Scientific Research

There is no relief in respect of commercial or residential land or buildings.

Differences in relief timing - The 100% first year allowance (e.g. for Plant and Machinery) can cause serious difficulties in double taxation relief matters.

20. Accountancy procedures and conventions

National and international accounting conventions are having an increasing effect on presentation of annual and periodic accounts. However, such alteration in accounting standards have little effect on United Kingdom Tax law (i.e. the law is not overriden by the accounting procedures).

21. Inflation Indices

The only area where inflation relief is given is in respect of trading stock and even that relief is subject to partial 'claw back'.

Tax relief by reference to inflation indices is not used in the United Kingdom.

The U.K. Government is awaiting firm pronouncements from the Accountancy Bodies before legislating in greater detail for relief on inflation factors.

22. Inventories

Measurement: Most methods of valuation which are related to cost, market or replacement values are acceptable for tax purposes. Nominal values or artificial lowering of values are not acceptable. The value for tax purposes can vary from value for accountancy purposes.

Increase in inventories - relief: This is 'stock relief' as mentioned in paragraph 21 above. The measure of increase relates to value and not to quantum.

23. Losses

Capital: If the asset is a chargeable asset for capital gains tax purposes, losses can be set against gains for the same period. Unused losses can be carried forward (no time limit).

23. Losses (cont'd)

Income: Trading income. Trading losses can be set against

i) Income (of whatever nature) and gains of the same period
then
ii) Income and gains of the preceding period
then
iii) Income from the specific trade (i.e. not any other trade) for future years.

Other income. Losses can only be used in the specific category of income (e.g. rental income losses can only be used as set off against other rental income for the same or subsequent periods).

24. Groups - reliefs etc. concepts

a) 51% holding enables dividends to be paid to parent without having an ACT payment. Later group interest can be paid without deducting withholding taxes.

b) 75% holding enables inter-company relief to be claimed for trading losses and management expenses. Capital assets can be transferred within the group free of capital gains.

c) 90% - owned by consortium - trading losses of the consortium-owned company can be relieved against profits of the consortium members.

25. Anti-avoidance

The main areas of legislation are:

i) Land Transaction
ii) Artificial relief for trading losses
iii) Transfers of shares giving a tax advantage
iv) Undue use of tax credits on dividend and interest payments
v) Transfer of assets abroad
vi) Transfer of businesses to places abroad
vii) Inter-company pricing

26. E.E.C. - Directives to date

27. Countries : Double Taxation Agreements

E.E.C.	Belgium	X
	Denmark	X
	France	X
	Federal Republic of Germany	X
	Holland	X
	Ireland	X
	Italy	X
	Luxembourg	X
Others in Europe		
	Portugal	X
	Spain	X
	Austria	X
	Norway	X
	Sweden	X
	Greece	X
	Switzerland	X
	Gibraltar	-
	Monaco	-
	Balkans	-

APPENDIX II

United Kingdom Company having branches

	France (Imputation system)	Holland (Classical System)	Germany (Split rate system)
Profit before tax	1,000	1,000	1,000
Company tax	500	480	430 140 (other taxes)
	500	520	430
Withholding tax	50	-	-
Taxed Income	450	520	430
Overseas tax total	£ 550	£ 480	£ 430
U.K. Tax on	1,000	1,000	860
@ 52% =	520	520	447
LESS Advance corporation tax on dividend of say £200	66	66	66
	454	454	381
Double Taxation Relief restricted to	454	454	381

This example ignores 'small companies' U.K. tax relief and assumes that the branch profit is the only source of U.K. income.

APPENDIX III

United Kingdom Company having Subsidiary Companies

	France	Holland	Germany	
Profits before tax	1,000	1,000	1,000	
Company tax	500	480	310 140	
	500	520	550	
Withholding Tax	30	30	110	
Taxed Income	470	490	440	
Overseas Tax Total	530	510	420	(assuming full distribution)
U.K. Tax on	1,000	1,000	860	
@ 52% =	520	520	520	
LESS Advance Corporation Tax on Dividend of say £200	66	66	66	
	454	454	454	
LESS Double Tax Relief restricted to	£ 454	£ 454	£ 454	

The Net Wealth Tax

Professor Dr. Hendrik Jan Hofstra
Retired Professor of Tax Law at the University of Leiden, former Minister of Finance of the Netherlands, The Hague

1. Taxes on property and wealth have a long history. In primitive societies, where wealth consisted mainly of land and real estate, taxes on land and buildings were not unusual; they existed already in Egypt, in Greece and Rome. The form was that of impersonal taxes ("Realsteuern" or "Objektsteuern"); their aim was mostly to tax the presumed yield of the property, not the value of the property itself. The notion of individual net wealth is much younger, dating from the time that merchants accumulated wealth in stocks and valuables and private bankers in loans to other people. In the beginning however the concept of individual wealth was vague and the tax-administration was unable to cope with the problems of a net wealth tax. In the Netherlands net wealth taxes during the seventeenth and eighteenth century appear as "extraordinaris" taxes - as one-time levies in the case of emergency -, but the repeated efforts proved to be just as many failures. After World War II a one-time tax on net wealth - net capital levy - was introduced, the proceeds of which were used to restore somewhat the financial chaos created by war and foreign occupation. The tax was sufficiently succesful, partly due to the fifty-years' experience with an annual net wealth tax acquired by the Dutch tax administration, and partly to special conditions of the post-war situation: full registration of all quoted shares and bonds, and extensive control on liquid assets and foreign currency.

These short remarks show that taxes on property and wealth in the past did assume divergent shapes. It may be added that in present times also taxation of property and wealth offers a far from uniform picture. The older form of an annual impersonal tax, mostly on real estate, persists in many countries, often reserved for the financing of provinces and municipalities. A net wealth tax exists in the Scandinavian countries, in Austria, Germany, Luxembourg, the Netherlands, and recently also in Spain, but not in the other countries belonging to the European Community. Combinations of different kind of taxes on property and wealth prevail. The survey is further complicated by the fact that the taxation of property and wealth may include other kinds of taxes: in addition to annual taxes on property and wealth in existence at a certain date - the annual property and net wealth taxes -, taxes on the movement or the transfer of property and wealth as well,i.e. the tax on transfer of real estate and, in a certain sense, also the death duties and gift tax. A third variety is the capital gains tax, being a tax not on the property itself but on the individual benefit obtained by the owner on the occasion of the realisation of the surplus-value. All these taxes are, regardless of their structure and character, related in this sense that a judgement on a separate tax has to take into account the other relevant taxes on property and wealth in the country concerned as well. Although the harmonisation of taxation within the European Community requires a common pattern, the history and socio-economic conditions of specific countries may therefore allow for deviations therefrom. It may be stated that up till now the E.C. Commission has no clear policy in relation to wealth taxes. The problem will however inevitably arise later, and it seems useful to start discussions at an early stage.

2. The characteristics of a net wealth tax differ widely from those of property taxes. The former is a personal tax, including in principle all assets of the taxpayer, after deduction of his debts and other liabilities; the latter are impersonal taxes on specific assets - mostly real estate -, charging the owner or benificiary, regardless of his other assets and ignoring the debts burdening the property. The switch from impersonal to personal taxes was the result of a change in the basic concepts of taxation during the 19th century.

The foundations of present-day tax systems in most developed countries were laid about 1900. Net wealth taxes, in the countries where they exist, usually date from the same period.

Until about 1930 tax systems were strongly influenced by the conceptions of Adam Smith. The background was Smith's view that government expenditure represents a collective consumption, the costs of which have to be borne - as the expenses of a big estate have to be borne by the joint tenants of that estate - by the joint taxpayers in accordance with their relative ability to pay. Smith's views however were not very clear, especially when advocating a taxation of individuals in proportion to the taxpayer's revenue. His concept of revenue was ambiguous. The discussion on the nature of personal income - instead of yield of a specific commodity - started only half a century after the "Wealth of nations" was published, and did not lead to generally accepted conclusions. The notion of taxation in proportion to the personal revenue or income was replaced by progressive income taxation, be it that the rate of progression remains arbitrary. Most important for the problem of net wealth taxation is the fact that the taxpayer's ability to pay depends on more elements than only his nominal income. The ability to pay of a married taxpayer is less than that of a single person having the same income, especially if the former in addition has to raise young children. Extraordinary expenses i.e. for serious illness, may further cut down the taxpayer's ability to pay. The possession of private wealth on the other hand strengthens the financial position of the taxpayer and may be assumed to represent an additional element in establishing his ability to pay. Notwithstanding Smith's ambiguities and the lack of clarity of his views ability to pay remained for a long period the leading principle in distributing the taxburden and in shaping the tax systems of the more developed countries. The dominating value of the ability-to-pay principle has somewhat diminished since the 1930's, by the introduction of other non-fiscal-elements into the tax systems: a point to which I will refer later. Nevertheless the conviction that a greater ability-to-pay imposes an obligation to pay greater contributions to the common needs still stands in present times as well.

3. Taxes are contributions to cover current government expenditure. Taxes have therefore in principle to be paid out of current income, and income is the best criterion of paying taxes according to ability to pay. I suggested however that the possession of wealth represents an additional autonomous -element of ability to pay; a statement which needs further explanation.

In the past, two considerations have been brought forward. The first is that income from investment tends to be more stable than income from labour; the second that the possession of wealth itself grants advantages to the owner not included in the concept of income: advantages by way of security- available wealth constitutes a reserve for emergencies and old age, for which the wage-earner has to save out of his taxable income-, advantages of opportunity, i.e. to acquire non taxable capital gains, and advantages of leisure, adding to his general wellbeing.

Depending on the importance attached to these considerations different solutions are possible. In concentrating on the presumed greater stability of investment income a distinction within the income tax can be made between investment income and so-called earned income, taxing the investment income at a higher rate than the earned income. The consequences of this approach however are scarcely acceptable. The system does not allow for an additional tax in relation to assets yielding no revenue within the meaning of income tax law. Thus the millionaire having no income in the legal sense -i.e. because he decides not to pay out dividends on his shares in a fully owned limited company or if he invests his money in non-profit yielding assets promising a non-taxable capital gain- escapes taxation although his ability to pay is much greater than that of a poor wage-earner. Secondly, if and when investment income is received, the additional tax due is related to the amount of income in stead of related to the net wealth. The shortcomings of this system are considerably strengthened by the deficiencies of the legal concept of income, opening numerous ways of tax avoidance. Actually the sense of wealth is to be found in the control over resources, adding to the capacity to pay tax. In the concept of ability to pay the taxation of wealth therefore can only be based on the wealth as such, justifying a net wealth tax as an inevitable supplement to the income tax.

4. It may be presumed that at the time when, in a number of countries, a net wealth tax was introduced, the tax was in accordance with the principles of prevailing taxation theory. The tax was not meant as a payment out of the wealth itself. Net wealth was only the taxbase. The net wealth tax should be paid out of income, in addition to the income tax levied at a moderate rate, in such a way that in principle income tax and net wealth tax together should not exceed the amounts considered to be reasonable. That under exceptional conditions -the millionaire mentioned before - net wealth tax would be due in the absence of income could be justified by the favoured treatment of capital gains. The rate of the tax was low - mostly between half of a percent and one percent of the net wealth- and practically proportional with a basic exemption (Bentham system). After some years of experience the administration of the tax proved to be fairly simple. Although the budgetary importance of the tax was -and is- relatively small, an additional advantage is that the tax provides a cross-check of some value on the administration of other taxes,i.e. income tax, death duties and gift tax.

5. The fact nevertheless that a net wealth tax exists only in a limited number of countries may be seen as a signal that arguments against a net wealth tax are not to be neglected. They are scarcely of an economic nature. It has been said that the net wealth tax may reduce the incentive to save Considering that the traditional net wealth tax is not an additional tax, but an alternative for other systems aiming at more heavily taxing investment income, the objection seems unjustified. The overall-possibilities of saving remain the same. If taxpayers want, at a given age, to possess a capital providing a certain net income after taxation, the net wealth tax may even force them -as is the case of an increase of income tax rates- to save more. The result therefore is uncertain, and at a low rate of the tax the consequences can scarcely be of importance; less important in every case than the check on working harder caused by higher income taxation. From the economic point of view the net wealth tax furthermore has the distinct advantages of discouraging the holding of liquid assets and -because the shifting of the tax is highly improbable- not leading to a rise of the pricelevel as may appear in the case of an

investment income surcharge. The latter advantage does not occur in so far as limited companies also are subject to a net wealth tax, which they will try to shift to consumers. The extension of the net wealth tax to limited companies, implying a double taxation of the shareholders if the shifting of the tax does not succeed, should however be rejected. The justification of the net wealth tax lies in the concept of ability to pay, being an idea which can be applied only to individuals. Subjecting limited companies to a net wealth tax therefore lacks theoretical backing. It is economically undesirable, because of the probability of shifting, and means a double taxation of the shareholders which cannot be justified.

The main arguments against the net wealth tax are to be found in its presumed practical difficulties. The concept of net wealth includes all kinds of assets -real estate and shares, bonds and other claims, furniture, jewellery and cars, pictures, books, collections of stamps, antiquities- less liabilities. Some of these assets, especially real estate, can easily be identified, but for other assets disclosure is more difficult or practically impossible. It has therefore been stated that the net wealth tax in practice is not able to tax the real wealth of a taxpayer and that its aim can only very imperfectly be realised. The second argument against the net wealth tax concerns the problem of valuation. The contention is that a yearly valuation of all assets is outside the scope of administrability and that all taxation of net wealth must therefore remain arbitrary.

A certain amount of truth in these objections has to be granted. They should however not be exaggerated. A fully perfect tax does not exist, has never existed and never will. If furthermore the justification of the net wealth tax is to be found in the additioned ability to pay emanating from the control of resources, certain assets, e.g. furniture, although perhaps expensive to buy, are not intended to be sold, and if they are scarcely obtain a selling price of any importance. On both theoretical and practical grounds they can therefore be omitted from the tax base, so that the objection fails. The same reasoning does not apply to valuable collections of a scientific or artistic character, but the promotion of science and the arts may justify the same exemption, either in full or up to a certain limit.

The first problem of administration is the control of taxable assets. I have already remarked that real estate, in a country where a complete registration of real estate (cadaster) exists, does not produce any difficulty. Difficulties may arise in the field of shares and bonds but they do not differ from those experienced already in the taxation of income. If a sufficient system of control can be worked out for the income tax -and in my opinion it must be possible - the solution for the net wealth tax is automatically given. The same applies to bank accounts, loans to other taxpayers, etc., and the participation in a business is known from the income tax returns. It may be conceded that a check on cash-balances -banknotes and coins- is practically impossible. Their importance however is relatively small, and greater amounts usually come to light when invested, in which case the legislation of most countries allows for a revised assessment of former years.

In the second place the problem of valuation has to be considered. The notion of value is open to more than one interpretation. If however the additional ability to pay of net wealth consists in the possibility of using assets for other purposes, value should be understood as the sellingprice to be obtained from the highest bidder, in selling under usual conditions.

The valuation of quoted shares and bonds -important species of relevant assets- does not present any difficulties. The value of a private business can be computed from the balance sheet, with necessary corrections if certain business assets are clearly underestimated. Here, as in the case of real estate,an important feature is that the rate of a net wealth tax, in the sense of a supplement to income tax, is rather modest. Practice in the countries where a net wealth tax exists is therefore that the administrative control is confined to a global one, without violation of the structure of the tax. The most difficult problem of valuation is that of non-quoted shares, especially in the case of a shareholder controlling the company. Experience however shows that in these cases too reasonable solutions can usually be arrived at, even if only after consultation with the taxpayer or by way of a compromise.

The assessment of net wealth tax mostly takes place annually - with the exception of Germany, where the assessment remains unchanged for a three years'period- , in the same office which deals with the taxpayer's income tax. A combined tax return for both taxes is usual. Actually the handling of the combined tax return does not take much more time than the control of a single income tax return. As I mentioned before,the information on the development of the taxpayer's net wealth may also be of some use in assessing income tax; information which would have to be acquired in some other way if net wealth tax did not exist.

The conclusion therefore may be that the practical and administrative complications of the tax are not such that they can qualify the theoretical neccessity of a net wealth tax in a tax system based on ability to pay.

6. The picture however would not be complete without giving attention to the changed role of taxation in the last quarter of a century, and to the relation of an annual net wealth tax with other taxes on property and wealth mentioned before.

It is clear that general tax theory lags far behind fiscal practice and actual social conditions. The fiscalist's real task for the time to come, in my opinion, is not to study specific problems of separate taxes, but to revise our basic conceptions on taxation. Present-day tax theory is still clinging to ability to pay as the main principle of taxation. Present-day practice however uses taxation as an instrument in supporting general policy, of which a reduction of differences in income and wealth is a not unimportant part. Thus we are faced, among many others, with the question whether a quite different type of net wealth taxation - viz. a tax aiming at reducing intentionally the bigger private fortunes- would not be preferable as part of general policy. Such a tax would have to charge the large fortunes at a progressive rate, leaving the question open what to do with the smaller ones. The answer is a matter of policy which cannot be discussed here, and a number of objections can be put forward, but the tandency in some countries to increase the rate of the net wealth tax accentuates the topicability of the problem.

Changes both in the social structure and in the tax systems of the Western world would on the contrary seem to point in quite the opposite direction. During the 19th century and the first quarter of the 20th century the higher stability of investment income compared with income from labour would be obvious, even if under those conditions the UK system of an income tax surcharge for investment income could scarcely be considered an efficient method of taxing the addional ability to pay: see earlier. Recent years however have not left much of the stability of investment income if inflation losses and capital losses are taken into account, and the social security and status of Adam Smith's "labouring poor" have improved considerably. Unemployment remains a great social and individual evil, but social-security systems provide allowances where labour income is lacking. The time that old age for the majority of the people automatically meant poverty and misery is past. Pension funds provide old age pensions, the value of which usually is not incorporated in the concept of net wealth. Labour laws and collective bargaining protect the employees against unjustified discharge. The advantage of possessing wealth remains, but the difference between investment income and earned income has decreased, and the advantage consists, as I remarked before, mainly in the wealth as such, and not in the income derived from it.

This is accentuated by the development of the level of taxation in general. During the period when high incomes mostly originated from wealth, the gap between the wealthy and the poor was great, and the rate of the income tax was low, an additional tax on wealth or investment income was necessary to meet real ability to pay. With income tax rates in some countries going up to 70 or 80%, the liability of income tax and a net wealth tax of more than 1% may however in combination easily exceed the income from investments. In the Netherlands, as in in a number of other countries, a regulation exists limiting the combined liability to 80% of the income enjoyed during the year. Theoretically this solution neglects the significance of wealth as an autonomous element of ability to pay. In practice the millionaire who has no income - or who succeeds, by using special constructions, in avoiding income taxation- does not have to pay net wealth tax either, although his ability to pay cannot be disputed. The better solution therefore is to restrict the rate of net wealth tax to a level where the situation in general does not arise. This means that the rate of the net wealth tax should be closely linked to the rate of the income tax and its actual burden. Where the latter remains relativity low a higher rate of the net wealth tax might be justified, as is problably the case in Spain, which has a rate of 2%. In countries where the top rate of the income tax exceeds 60 or 70% however a rate below 1% - probably not more than ½%- would be advisable.

7. The contribution of a net wealth tax to the needs of the Treasury, levied at the suggested modest rate, and - because of the necessary basic exemptions for small fortunes- burdening only a relatively small number of taxpayers, is not great: in the Netherlands the tax, even after the temporary increase of the rate to 0,8%, covers less than 1% of the budget. Although the administration of the tax does not offer serious difficulties -see earlier-, the question remains nevertheless whether its main aim - viz. promoting horizontal equity and justice - cannot be achieved more easily by using other means, especially a capital gains tax or death duties.

Disregarding for the moment the practical consequences it may first be stated that the character of those taxes differs widely from that of a net wealth tax. A net wealth tax is a yearly tax levied on the wealth existing at a certain point of time. The capital gains tax is a tax on the appreciation of the value of assets over a period of time; mostly, as I remarked before, a tax on the individual benefit obtained by the owner on the occasion of the realisation of the surplus-value. Capital gains may be included in the legal concept of income, and should be included according to the theories of Schanz - Haig - Simons..If they are not, but are subjected to a capital gains tax, the capital gains tax is not intended to tax the original wealth itself which is even excluded from the tax base, but to take into account an increased ability to pay escaping income taxation. The capital gains tax, in other words, can in relation to certain accretions of purchasing power be an alternative for income tax, but never for a tax on capital or wealth.

More complex is the connection between net wealth tax and death duties, particularly because death duties exist in different forms, and their justification is not always the same. Two types prevail: estate duty and inheritance tax. In a tax system based on ability to pay the inheritance tax seems the more logical, as in the conception that death duties should reduce inequalities of wealth. In both cases -compare the definition of income of Schanz - Haig - Simons - the tax is more akin to an income tax than to a tax on capital or wealth, and the conclusion drawn in relation to the capital gains tax applies as well. This is accentuated by the fact that the rates of the inheritance tax in practically all countries differ according to the family relation between deceased and heir. The surviving spouse and the children of the deceased mostly enjoy a privileged rate; distantly related persons have to pay at a much higher rate. Especially if widow, widower or children- as has been repeatedly advocated: a question on which I will not dwell - can claim a full exemption, the inheritance tax, being zero, cannot be a substitute for the net wealth tax which the deceased should have paid.

The estate tax on the contrary is a tax on the capital or wealth left by the deceased. There the question could be raised whether a one-time tax on the occasion of death is not preferable to the administration of a yearly tax at a lower rate. But here also there is no fixed relation between the accumulated wealth tax liability during the lifetime of a taxpayer and the estate duty liable on the occasion of his decease. One taxpayer lives to be a hundred years of age; in other cases the same estate may pass over several times within a short period. Whatever the justification of an estate duty may be, as an alternative to an annual net wealth tax also the estate duty acts too arbitrarily to be acceptable.

8. In my preceding remarks some of the technicalities of the net wealth tax have already been discussed. Some final remarks may be useful to complete a global picture.

Following the usual income tax treatment of investment income the traditional tax unit for wealth tax purposes is the family. The tax base is the combined wealth of husband and wife, and in several countries the wealth of minor children is included as well. The consequence is that a married couple is entitled to a higher personal exemption - a higher threshold- than a single person, and that in the latter case child allowances have to be granted.

I will not deny that I have serious doubts about the family being treated as tax unit for income tax purposes. In my opinion changing views on the position of women indicate some kind of income splitting, and children of a certain age should be treated independently. This however is a problem outside the scope of this lecture, and as long as the income tax treatment of the family income remains unchanged, the pattern seems acceptable for the net wealth tax as well.

In discussing the practical objections against a net wealth tax I stressed already the desirability of exempting furniture and personal effects from the tax base, including jewellery for personal use up to a certain amount; cars and boats however in most countries are taxable objects.
It may be granted that the exemption favours taxpayers investing in expensive furniture, in stead of income yielding assets, but practical considerations in this case have to overcome theoretical objections.

Assets not yielding a cash income also include owner-occupied houses. They present a double problem. The first question - viz. whether they should be included in the tax base or not - has to be answered in the affirmative.
The owner occupied house has a value like other houses. In many cases the house represents even the main asset of the taxpayer. The ability to pay of a taxpayer having a certain income and a house of his own

is clearly higher than that of a taxpayer having the same income without owning a house. This may affect his income tax liability, but means also that he has wealth at his disposal. The second question relates to the valuation of the property. Social reasons, and the fact that the owner occupied house represents in most cases a permanent abode not intended to be sold, may induce to a somewhat favoured treatment. Different solutions are, if desired, feasible, generally without creating serious administrative complications.

A major problem, which did not yet arise at the time when most net wealth taxes were introduced, is the treatment of pension rights and similar provisions. The taxpayer without pension rights has to save out of his income after paying income tax to provide for his old age. The taxpayer taking part in an adequate pension scheme can spend the total of his income without worrying about the future. Pension rights may have a considerable value, in some cases up to say ƒ1.000.000,-- Practice however is that they are left out of the concept on net wealth, whereas the taxpayer without pension rights who has saved up the same amount out of his income, has to pay net wealth tax thereon.

There is of course a difference between wealth in the form of marketable real estate or quoted shares and pension rights, the value of which in general cannot be realized in ready cash. Pension rights therefore do not represent actual control of resources, on which the net wealth tax rests. Neglecting pension rights in shaping the tax structure nevertheless interferes unacceptably with horizontal equity as between taxpayers with and without such rights.

The solution can be found in two ways. The first is to include the value of pension rights in the concept of net wealth. The yearly valuation of those rights however presents unsurmountable difficulties, not mentioning the fact that the administration of the tax would extend to numerous persons having no wealth outside their pension rights. The other solution is to grant an additional personal exemption to taxpayers without pension rights or sufficient pension rights.It is this solution that on reasons of horizontal equity I would suggest. A relatively arbitrary set of rules will be neccessary, dependant on the age of the taxpayer, but the consequence could be to raise somewhat the rate of the tax applicable to the remaining wealth. Pension type annuities and life insurance policies, which nowadays are usually exempted, could be treated as pension rights.

The international aspects of the tax - to mention a last point- offer no difficulties.Subjects of the tax are private persons residing in the country on their net wealth, wherever situated, and non-residents on property situated in the country. To avoid double taxation however residents may enjoy an exemption for assets liable to tax in other countries, in accordance with provisionsof double taxation agreements or autonomous statutes, the latter in general following the same pattern as suggested by the well-known draft convention of the OECD.

9. To summarise I may suggest the following conclusions.

A. the possession of net wealth by private persons constitutes an autonomous factor of ability to pay, independent of the income derived from it.

B. A tax system valuing ability to pay cannot neglect this factor. The annual net wealth tax is theoretically superior to an income tax surcharge on investment income. Capital gains tax and death duties, based on quite different assumptions,are unable to act as a substitute.

C. Administration and control of the tax are sufficiently easy and there is no need to reject the theoretically correct solution on practical grounds.

D. The notion of ability to pay applies only to private persons, not to corporations. A case for a net wealth tax on corporations cannot be made.

E. The net wealth tax should act as a supplement to income tax. Viewing the prevailing progressive rates of income taxation the rate of the tax should be proportional or slightly progressive, and modest - in general not exceeding ½ to 1% -, with a threshold exempting small fortunes.

F. Household and personal effects should be exempted, and the law should contain a special provision in favour of taxpayers not entitled to pension rights, pension type annuities or similar claims for old age.

G. For the time being married couples should be liable to tax on their combined net wealth.

H. Residents of the country are subject to the tax on their total net wealth - with provisions to avoid double taxation in the case of property liable to tax abroad - and non-residents on property situated in the country.

Discussion

Prof. Dr. Albert Tiberghien, President of the C.F.E. (Belgium)

My warmest thanks for your remarkable and complete paper. I would just like to add that Mr. Hofstra just finished three or four months ago, the famous report which he wrote for the Dutch government on the adaptation of taxation to inflation. This report has been a great success in Holland and in the other countries and it is a great pity that our Congress is so short, otherwise I would have asked Mr. Hofstra to speak on his report. This would certainly have been highly interesting.

Mr. Jan W. Bettinck, Belastingadviseur (Netherlands)

As far as I know, there is no wealth tax in the United Kingdom. Prof. Hofstra has been a steady critic for years on the "ability to pay", he is not doing so for the first time here today. He has also said that we may expect to witness the end of the "ability to pay" principle. This principle is not obsolete. He spoke of the social revolution of the last 25 years. In my view, Prof. Hofstra has greatly criticized wealth tax, so that we are left with only one conclusion nowadays, namely that a wealth tax as we know it, has become obsolete. I think that the comments made by Prof. Hofstra from a) to e) are correct, but only if one basically accepts wealth tax. I feel that the principle of wealth tax should be thought over, just as Prof. Hofstra stated.

Mr. Gert Sass (EC-Commission)

I would just like to come back to a comment made by Prof. Hofstra, which concerns the concept of the Commission regarding the question of wealth tax. As head of the department for direct taxes, I feel of course particulary called to do so. Prof. Hofstra is certainly right with his comment. Of course, it is necessary if one speaks of the future taxation of companies within the EC - as has been the case this morning - that one also gives wealth tax some thought. If Mr. Burke just now, and Mr. Hendriksen this morning, did not speak in detail of wealth tax, this is just because they felt that the other questions were of far greater immediate interest. Let me just make three short comments:

1. Wealth tax is certainly only of relative importance, if one thinks of competition among companies within the common market. This was clearly said by Prof. Vogel and by Prof. Hofstra. Wealth tax is levied only in Germany and in Luxembourg, mainly in the case of corporations, which are concerned with international competition. Only natural persons are levied in Denmark, Holland and Ireland.
2. On the basis of the explanations given this morning, it seems that we want to give taxes on profits and income, priority as regards the order in which harmonization of direct taxes is tackled. It seems obvious that there is little point in trying to harmonize taxes other than those on profits and income, before those on profits and income

themselves have been harmonized. It was apparent also this morning, just how complicated and long-winded this road is. The directive on corporation taxes has been submitted. The next step is that of the regulations concerning the determinations of profits, and the determination of the tax base for corporation taxes. This has been expressly requested by Prof. Hofstra this morning. The third step would be the tax rates. If you remember, just how long it has taken already in the case of the regulations concerning the determination of profits, the problem of the measures of incentives will certainly not be dealt with in one go, from one day to the next. If you think of the various rates of inflation within the Common Market and finally think of the difficulty of the regulations serving to determine profits, then you realize that this can certainly not be brought about in less than two years. It will only be at the end, as a third step, that one can start thinking of the rates. Wealth tax, just like all the other taxes, other than those on profits and income should only be dealt with when the tax burden of corporations themselves is in question, that is to say only when the question of rates is discussed.

3. There is no point of course in what seems to be either the medium or the long term, to start thinking about what should be done with wealth tax: Should it be introduced in a uniform way within the EC for enterprises or should it be done away with?

Prof. Dr. Horst Vogel, Steuerberater and Rechtsanwalt (Germany)

Prof. Hofstra, you have held an excellent pladoyer against the levying of a net wealth tax on companies or on joint stock companies, stating that in your view there is no justification in a double tax burden. Only those who hold shares should be taxed. I would just like to draw your attention to the fact that the problem is then far more complex, when you have - as is the case in the Federal Republic of Germany - 90 % of companies in the form of private companies. I would just like to add that a net wealth tax, if it is generally introduced, would considerably reduce the propensity and capacity to invest, in view of the economic problems which we have to expect. I feel that net wealth tax represents a greater danger for investments, in particular, as is the case in our country, when it is coupled with other wealth taxes, such as in Germany, the tax on trade capital. A levying of a net wealth tax on investments, if no profit has been made, is desastrous. It corresponds to an anti-investments tax. For this reason I would like to warn the other seven states of the EEC, and perhaps one day there might be twelve, not to follow the example given by Luxembourg and the Federal Republic of Germany and to introduce a net wealth tax. For, Ladies and Gentlemen, today we have already reached the point where investments in a company, already give a smaller yield than investments in government bonds. And this is not only the case, in the Federal Republic of Germany, it is already the case in France, in Great Britain and even in the USA. If the yield from an investment in a commercial company, which is tied to a far greater risk, already brings in a smaller yield than government bonds, then this will annihilate the spirit of commercial enterprise. At that point it is no longer worth while. Furthermore, if a net wealth tax is levied, which does not take the profit into account, then this will be fatal for the economy.

Dr. Franz Hörstmann, Steuerberater (Germany)

The topic which you have just dealt with, Prof. Hofstra, is in fact a topic which concerns tax reformers rather than tax consultants. I used to belong to a Commission of tax reformers. So as to give you an answer immediately, I would have had to keep up with the whole business of tax reform. A paper on this topic would have been extremely interesting. I found the examples given were slightly far-fetched. Wage earners are not always poor people - you spoke of poor wage earners -, and the risks associated with wealth are often, and I might even add, as a general rule, greater than the risks associated with a working wage. Because there is a lesser risk, you gave this as a reason, a tax should be levied on it. This gives me ground for second thoughts.

We are agreed that wealth tax, is a tax on a particularly solid income. But what happens, if this wealth does not yield any profit? The millionaire who is free to determine, at will, that he shall have no yield on his wealth and who invests his wealth only so as to have a rise in value of his wealth, is no doubt a rare exception. I know 50 millionaires, but none of that kind. As a general rule, millionaires go to the greatest trouble, to make use of their wealth, so that it gives employment and yields a result. The other type, that of the speculator, there may have been some of those, one meets them from time to time even today. But these are not typical examples. The typical situation is the one which Prof. Vogel has just described. Indeed, companies pay the greatest part of the wealth tax burden, namely 80 %, and must furthermore pay other taxes when they have made a profit. If such a company has the misfortune to work at a loss during three or four years in succession, then wealth tax can be fatal and give rise to a considerable loss of jobs. So far, we thought, that we were the only ones to carry the cross of wealth tax, here in the Federal Republic of Germany. But if the other countries also have to carry that cross, this would then solve the problem from the point of view of international competition. Nevertheless, it seems to me one cannot go on explaining wealth tax for companies with the argument that it is a tax on a particularly solid income. In that case it would be better to tax the income, if the wealth has a yield, rather than the capital itself if there is no yield.

We all feel that this tax should be eliminated.

Mr. Winfried Wachter, Steuerberater (Germany)

It is interesting to note that those who took part in the discussion so far have all spoken against wealth tax. I do not wish to repeat the arguments which have been made against wealth tax. I feel, nevertheless, that a discussion on the introduction of a net wealth tax should take situation to-day into account. I would like to say a few words on the situation in the Federal Republic of Germany. We have been forced, following the recession, to hold a very detailed discussion on the effects of taxes other than those on profits and income. It has been said that wealth tax is a tax on a particularly solid income. What is a "solid income"? It has been pointed out in the Federal Republic of Germany, that incomes which in general are considered "solid", for example, the income on the company capital of an individual enterprise, or the share in a private company, are particularly endangered incomes, because the wealth which yields the income is particularly endangered itself. If these are burdened with taxes other than those on profits and income, it has been shown, in our so delicate economic situation, that the dangers become enormous. This is the line of thought in discussions in Germany. We have strongly felt the negative effects. So much on the question of "solid income".

If Mr. Hofstra said that this net wealth tax was not applicable to moral persons, this is only thanks to double taxation. All the other arguments, however, apply to individual companies and private companies of both commercial and professional nature. Double taxation alone concerns only moral persons. One should examine the possibility of drawing a line between net wealth tax as applied to moral persons and the taxation of the so-called "solid income" of commercial enterprises. It should furthermore be taken into account that it is not possible to come to terms with the inflationary increase of the nominal values in the case of net wealth tax. On the one hand nominal values are taxed, namely in the case of net wealth tax and on the other hand it will prove difficult to evaluate certain wealth values with nominal values, for example, landed estate. If it is attempted to adapt landed estate to nominal values this will directly lead to a tax burden on wealth, which the land owners will no longer be able to meet. In such a case separate tax rates, or something similar, will have to be introduced, which will certainly not help to simplify these taxes, which are supposedly easy to levy. If land is taxed with nominal values and if rates ranging between 0,5 % and 1 % are applied, then the net wealth tax could easily reach a point of ressemblance with expropriation. There is absolutely no doubt that the same applies to individual enterprises and shares in private companies. In situations of medium term losses, the net wealth tax has an expropriation character. We would like to give due warning on the grounds of the experience which we have made with this tax.

Regarding the argument of the ease and cheapness of levy: It could be that there are systems which enable an easier and cheaper levy of net wealth tax than the system applied in the

Federal Republic of Germany. Our experience, at any rate, has shown that the evaluation or the setting of the values alone, not the levying of the tax, for example, for land the evaluation of the whole premises, represents in the Federal Republic of Germany a considerable amount of administrative work, which if only applied to net wealth tax - but this applies luckily to a number of other taxes, certainly surpasses the yield itself out of net wealth tax. On the whole regarding the question of net wealth tax, care should be given and the outcome of the last discussion, in particular concerning the principle of nominal values under inflation, the principle of nominal values in the case of landed estate and the costs should be very carefully examined and should only be accepted, if a definitly positive solution is reached. Our experience has shown that the opposite is true.

Mr. Karl Krammig, Steuerberater (Germany)

During the 15 years in which I have been politically active as Member of Parliament in the Finance Committee of the German Bundestag, I have learnt that everyone, who speaks in favour of a tax, judges the tax in relation to the capacity of payment of the citizens. If one takes each tax individually, this leads to a permanent decrease of the capacity of payment. It shall soon no longer be necessary to levy taxes when the capacity for payment has been completely devoured.

Prof. Dr. Hendrik Jan Hofstra (Netherlands)

I have gove into the advantages and disadvantages of a net

wealth tax. It has not been said that we should again have a net wealth tax. Nor, to my mind, must we say that we cannot have it. I have made a difference between net wealth tax for moral persons and net wealth tax for natural persons. I have said that net wealth tax for moral persons is unfair, as also that applied to commercial capital. On the other hand it has been said, also by you, Prof. Vogel, that if a tax is levied without there having been a profit, this will weaken the enterprises so much that one can call it irresponsible. I have based my paper on opinions which, I feel, are still on the whole accepted today. At least in Holland, in my country, if one listens to tax discussions in Parliament one realizes that everything is explained with the argument of the capacity of payment. Be it that the argument of the capacity of payment is used for or against the tax. No one knows what it means. I have underlined the fact that those who do not belong to a pension scheme, must be allowed an added tax free amount, so that the land owner has perhaps his 100 000 DM free of tax already secured. So that when he reaches the age of 45 or 50 he will have an equivalent to make up for the absence of pension sheme. In this way wealth tax is applied to the larger wealths.

I may have done the European Commission wrong, when I said that it had not yet reached harmonization. I have made note of this and I suppose that the Commission will get around to it in good time. I agree, I think, with the statement made by Prof. Vogel as also with Prof. Tiberghien's statement, the next speaker. Mr. Wachter also stressed the same points. I must admit that the values for landed estate have considerably risen, also in my country. When I was still working with the Tax Authorities, 100 Gulden was a good price for 3 acres, now they are worth 40 000 Gulden. The tax values have certainly not kept up with this trend in Holland. I think that estimations remain far below the true value, which of course is theoretically unfair. Mr. Wachter's experience that estimations are so difficult in Germany is certainly true, I am not acquainted with the German experience, but in my country - perhaps we do not want to go as far as the last drop - things are working out quite well. According to my personel experience, and that is already a few years ago, the added information which can be collected on the basis of a yearly declaration of wealth, serves as a mesure of control on income. It can of course be argued that it could be included in income law, which would mean that not only should a declaration of income be made, but also a statement of wealth. In this way the same result would be reached. Members of Parliament are already acquainted with this, and I have been a member of Parliament for 15 years. That will never be done. If there is a net wealth tax, consequently the wealth situation has to be disclosed.

Prof. Dr. Albert Tiberghien, President of the C.F.E. (Belgium)

Many thanks, Mr. Hofstra, for your statement. Let us however not forget that we are not here to carry on the politics of our own country but that we have got together here to think together, just as in a conclave, on important fiscal problems, so as to shake the big fiscal tree, to see what falls and what doesn't, what is solid and what isn't. This is what Mr. Hofstra expressed so well. He said that he did not write this study as a politician, but as a man of learning.

Cooperation in the Field of Tax Consulting between Members of the Same and of Different Liberal Professions

Professor Dr. Jos Jan Couturier
Conseil Fiscal, Antwerp

Translated from French by Roselle Prill du Pradal

I. Introduction

Western European way of life has greatly changed since the beginning of the century. This change, enhanced by the enormous progress of science, has not left the practice of so-called liberal professions untouched. Hence, in the medical, paramedical and technical world practioners work more and more as specialized teams. The traditional picture of the individual profession is disappearing.

Representatives of the liberal professions belonging to the economic and legal sectors have not escaped from the social trend which is taking shape. As far as they are concerned, this trend is characterized by the fact that the number of regulations has not ceased to increase, new regulations are increasingly complicated, changes brought about in the texts in force are more and more frequent, and as a consequence of the interference by existing regulations, by new regulations and by changes which affect the whole, the field of activity is so extensive and so complex that one man alone can no longer keep up with it.

According to the classical model, the rendering of services by an independent individual, working on his own, to a limited number of individual clients, who had confidence that we had availed of a specific intellectual education, was characteristic of a liberal profession. The professional enjoyed complete liberty in his work, including that of setting his own fees, but he imposed upon himself a high standard of professional ethics and carried considerable personal responsibility. Towards his clients, he acted in an unbiased and non-businesslike way; towards his colleagues, he had respect for the rule of perfect equality. This model probably corresponded to the demands of social life during the 19th century, but it no longer seems to comply with the needs of society today.

Since the number of regulations has not ceased to grow, an increasing number of persons feel the need to refer to a specialist a growing number of increasingly diverse and complex problems. And because of the frequency of amendments, they must be inclined to reexamine constantly problems which had already been solved. The individual professional thus finds himself faced with the insurmountable task of keeping up to date and of increasing without respite the profiency he had initially acquired. The solution does not reside in an ever increasing specialization since many legal and economic problems simultaneously affect many different professional disciplines. To this problem one can add the fact that clients are increasingly extending their activity beyond frontiers. The individual professional is thus faced with a new challenge, yet more extensive than the preceding ones: that of mastering foreign regulations.

It is obvious that cooperation has become a must, not only among representatives of the same profession, such as lawyers, notaries, chartered accountants, tax concultants, but also among representatives from different disciplines, if not from all of them, belonging to appropriate professional associations.

This does not only apply to the national level, but also to the international level.

It is out of question that one man alone practise with success two or more of the professions with which we are concerned. It is out of question that one tax consultant alone keep abreast with all the taxation systems, that of his own country as well as that of the other countries of the Community. It is even out of question that he should be able to master all the aspects of his national system of taxation, both direct and indirect. Since the interpenetration of economic activity has become a reality within each Member State and within the Community taken as a whole, would it not be a good solution to establish pluri-disciplinary offices for lawyers (barristers, legal consultants, notaries), chartered accountants and tax consultants, where the different specialists would work side by side and supplement each other and would be assured of the direct cooperation of foreign specialists? Thus a German client who wished to create an establishment in France could find assistance both in France and in Germany from a group of specialists: in Germany for legal questions related to the planned extension in France by a notary who would pass the necessary deeds, by a legal consultant for the interpretation of the law on business practice, by an accountant for the organization and keeping of accounts and by a tax consultant for taking care of the tax situation arising out of the opening of a business in France.

This present paper aims at examining, after a brief introduction to the professions that concern us, the rules (laws, regulations, ethical codes) governing these professions, so as to assess to what extent cooperation is possible among tax consultants on the one hand, among tax consultants and the members of other liberal professions on the other, both on the national and international level.

II. The various professions in each of the respective countries

A. Examination of the possibility of a competent taxation assistance

The gulf between the traditional way that many lawyers and notaries have continued to practise theire profession, and the needs of the business world has left room for new professions, e. g. the tax consultant. Assistance given by professionals in the field of taxation must entail, if it is to be complete, the carrying out of writings (tax declarations and other deeds) and the representation of the tax payer before the administrative authorities and the judiciary. From what follows it shall be seen that tax consultants are not everywhere in a position to provide all of these services.

1. Countries where the profession of the tax consultant is governed by a legal régime

a. Federal Republic of Germany

In no other country of the Community is the profession of the tax consultant so fully organized as in the Federal Republic of Germany. The activity of the tax consultant (Steuerberater) is regulated by a special law (Steuerberatungsgesetz). It consists of counselling tax payers and of appearing for them before tax authorities. Particularly in that latter respect, the Steuerberater, an individual person or a legal entity, is authorized to appear for his clients not only before fiscal administrations, but also in the courts adjudicating upon fiscal matters (Finanzgerichte and Bundesfinanzhof). Since 15 September 1975, the tax payer must be represented by a professional in the Supreme Federal Court (Bundesfinanzhof). Only tax consultants (Steuerberater), barristers (Rechtsanwälte) and chartered accountants (Wirtschaftsprüfer) are entitled to appear.

Transitory measures determine the rights of fiscal mandates (Steuerbevollmächtigten) on this point.

On the other hand, the help given by tax consultants includes the carrying out of accountancy procedures as provided for by law and the drawing up of the balance sheet. Although definite bounds are set to the field of activity of the Steuerberater in accountancy matters, the German legislator sees no objections that the profession of the tax consultant (Steuerberater) and chartered accountant (Wirtschaftsprüfer) are exercised by the same person, as long as the holder fulfils the necessary conditions for both professions, taken individually.

Professional practice itself is governed by directives issued by the Federal Chamber of Tax Consultants (Bundessteuerberaterkammer) (professional directives). To become a member of the profession one must have passed an examination set by the Chamber. All who have a diploma or professional certificate, either from a faculty of Law or of Economics or from a vocational school, Institute or Technical College may sit the examination. Furthermore, candidates must have had sufficient professional experience acquired during a certain number of years, depending on the basic educational degree. The following are granted a dispensation from sitting the examination: University professors, judges from the fiscal tribunals and former employees and higher civil servants of the revenue department and of the legislative bodies, provided they have had suffiently long professional experience in the field of taxation. The nomination is in the hands of the highest authorities of the Laender ("Finanzministerium" or "Senat").

On account of the conditions necessary to become a member of the profession, and since the illegal practice of the profession is penalized, the title of tax consultant (Steuerberater) is well protected in the Federal Republic of Germany. The profession is fully practised and covers all the services a tax consultant can offer. It is true that certain parts of their competence must be shared with members of other professions such as the barristers (Rechtsanwälte) or the chartered accountants (Wirtschaftsprüfer), but this does not take away from its scope.

b. France

In France, the use of the title of legal advisor, of legal and tax advisors, or simply of tax consultants, is ruled by the law of December 31st, 1971, which reformed certain judicial and legal professions, including that of barristers. One should note that this law foresaw the possibility of unifying the professions of barrister and of legal advisor and established a commission which was to examine the appropriate measures. This commission has completed its study. The unification which had been planned was not brought about, neither in the form of one profession absorbing another, nor in the form of both professions converging towards one another with a view to becoming a new one. This last alternative is worth considering for the future. For the moment it is up against serious practical and structural problems. Law defines a legal advisor as a person who gives professional advice or who executes deeds for others in legal matters. The legal advisor, a natural or a moral person, is entitled to give any advice, draw out all private deeds for others and carry out all the formalities which follow from or accompany these acts, and can assist his clients in writing their declarations, statements, replies and various documents which are to be sent to public authorities or any public or private entities. Unless expressly prohibited by law or regulation, he may assist and represent the parties concerned before the public authorities and public and private entities. Although only barristers are in principal entitled to assist or represent their parties, plead and conduct suits in the law courts and before jurisdictional or disciplinary bodies, legal advisors are also admitted when the law permits assistance and representation through an authorized agent.

The use of the title of legal advisor or tax consultant, with or without an addendum indicating a specialization, is authorized only after enrollment on a list established by the Solicitor General.

The legal advisor must fulfil the same conditions of moral standing as the barrister. He must hold either a Masters in Law, or titles or diplomas recognized as equivalents for the practice of the profession in question. Furthermore, he must have had a practical professional experience of at least three years. Those who wish to use the title of tax consultant must fulfil stronger conditions of moral standing, have had a special professional education and show that they have had sufficient professional practice in the field of taxation.

A juristic person wishing to use the title, with or without an addendum indicating a specialization, will have to abide by a certain number of specific rules.

The enrollment on a list of legal advisors is not compatible with either belonging to the bar, or with the enrollment on the board of the "Ordre des Experts Comptables et des Comptables Agréés", or with the functions of public or ministry officer. It is also incompatible with all salary paid work, with the exception of that of associate of another legal advisor.

The legal advisor is entitled to exercise his profession throughout the national territory. However, the opening of another office for clients is permitted only within the judicial district of the Court of Appeals where the professional domicile or headquarters of the legal advisor is located.

The organization proper of the profession is carried out by regional commissions and a national commission of legal advisors, established by the decree of 15 March 1978.

2. Countries where the profession of the tax consultant is not legally organized

a. Italy

In Italy, the Tax Consultants' profession as such is not organized or protected by law. Anyone may give advice on taxation matters. The barristers hold the monopoly of representation before the tribunals, the Courts of Appeals and the Supreme Court. The assistance and representation of parties before the fiscal commissions and the central Commission can be assumed not only by barristers, but also by accountants, chartered accountants, geometricians, engineers, architects, and certified agricultural building and industrial experts, provided they are enrolled on the respective professional lists and have been granted authorization to do so by the Ministry for Finance. Thus the profession of tax consultant (tributariste) is mostly exercised within the professions named above. It can also be practised by civil servants belonging to the fiscal authorities who are enrolled on a special list drawn up by the Ministry. The formation of associations or of societies among professionals is generally admissible as long as the rules concerning the qualifications and individual responsability of the associates are respected.

b. Other countries

The profession of tax consultant is not organized to any greater degree in the other countries of the Community. In general, the tax payer has the choice of either fulfilling his fiscal obligations himself and of appearing before the revenue departments, or of being represented there by a duly authorized person. According to law, the latter need not fulfil any particular conditions. In these countries, anyone can become a tax consultant and work in that capacity. To which extent these persons can assist or represent tax payers before judicial bodies, depends upon the degree of monopoly conceded to other liberal professions. In the Netherlands, for example, only barristers may plead before the Supreme Court (Hoge Raad), to the exclusion even of the parties. In these countries it has been sought to organize the profession within private professional Unions.

In the Netherlands, there is the Order of Tax Consultants (Nederlandse Orde van Belastingconsulenten), the Federation of Tax Consultants (Nederlandse Federatie van Belastingconsulenten) and the Brotherhood of Tax Consultants (Broederschap van Belastingconsulenten), in the United Kingdom "The Institute Of Taxation". Professional Unions are also well established in Ireland, Denmark and Belgium.

The statutes of these professional unions recognize various categories of members. Admission to membership is made dependent upon a certain number of conditions such as the holding of a particular diploma or successful participation in the programme of professional education organized by the union itself. Most unions demand a certain professional experience, acquired either in the independent exercise of the profession, or as the associate of an independent tax consultant, or when working for a company, taxation matters having been the respective main field of work.

Furthermore, these members must abide by certain fixed rules as regards the practising of the profession itself. But they are also granted certain rights, such as the use of a joint trade mark in their correspondence. For example, the Dutch Federation of Tax Consultants has registered a joint trade mark at the Benelux Trade Marks Office, and the initials

AITI are reserved for the exclusive use of the Associates of the Institute of Taxation in Ireland.

Lastly, the professional unions pursue the objective of promoting the professional interests of their members with the government. Efforts are being made to arrive at a legal organization of the profession which would give the title of tax consultant legal protection.

B. A few words on the other professions

1. Chartered accountants, auditors and company auditors

Accounting professionals play a twofold role in the countries under study.

On the one hand, they have to carry out a control of accounts with the object of merely listing economic facts for the use of all those who are interested in the company life of companies. They must therefore be competent and independent persons of integrity.

On the other hand, they have to advise company executives basing themselves on the analysis they have carried out by means of accounting techniques, concerning the situation and operation of the company.

In most countries, accounting is generally practised by a number of professions. Some of these professions enjoy a legally protected title and the law reserves for them certain functions which are sometimes exclusive. This applies to auditors in France and company auditors in Belgium. They exercise their profession in a legally established framework which controls their training and ensures the permanent organization of a body of capable specialists (Compagnie Nationale des Commissaires aux Comptes en France, Institut des Réviseurs d'Entreprises en Belgique).

In all countries private professional associations defend the professional interests of the chartered accountants. In general, a certain theoretical training as well as certain practical experience are the necessary requirements of the profession. Prior practical experience is not, however, indispensable in the Grand Duchy of Luxemburg and in the Netherlands, nor in Italy, as far as the Dottori Commercialisti are concerned.

In the countries where the tax consultants profession is not legally organized, no legal provisions prevent the ordinary chartered accountant from giving counsel in the field of taxation. In Germany (Wirtschaftsprüfer), and to a certain extent in Italy (Ragioneri e Periti Commerciali, Dottori Commercialisti), the chartered accountant may even assist and represent the tax payer at some or all judicial bodies that adjudicate in taxation matters. In other countries, he comes up against the privileges of other professions, especially that of the bar. In France, there is even a legal incompatibility between the enrollment on the list of chartered accountants and the practising of the profession of legal advisor and/or tax consultant.

2. Barristers (avocats)

Since long ago, the barristers' profession enjoys in each of the countries under study vast privileges in the field of assistance and representation of parties before the judicial bodies. Of course, they have also the right to advise and to represent clients before public authorities, also in fiscal matters.

Their right to plead for clients in court, including fiscal matters, is exclusive in Belgium, Denmark, France and in the Grand Duchy of Luxembourg, apart from certain well defined exceptions.

In the Anglo-Saxon countries, which differentiate between barristers and solicitors, only barristers have the right to appear before the higher courts (Circuit Court in Ireland, High Court in the United Kingdom). On the other hand, only solicitors have the right to appear before certain lower courts.

In the Federal Republic of Germany, non-authorized persons who give legal or fiscal advice are liable to penalty. Let us just recall that in fiscal matters, the right to assist the tax payer and to appear for him in court is also held by the Steuerberater and the Wirtschaftsprüfer.

Let us also recall that in Italy, the monopoly held by the barristers only applies to the first instance courts, to the courts of appeal and to the supreme court, whereas members of other professions working on questions can also appear before the central commission and the tax commissions.

Finally, Dutch legislation grants the barrister a position of monopoly in civil law matters. In principle, the parties must be represented in court, but in fiscal matters they have a choice. They may either defend their case themselves or ask another person to represent them, and this representation is subject to no particular condition.

In all the countries concerned, the profession of barrister (avocat) is legally organized except in Ireland where the rules are determined by tradition.

3. Notaries

Due to their public function, notaries must intervene whenever required by law, and also in those cases where the parties concerned want to give the exact legal form to the deeds they have drawn up.

Originally, notaries seemed to devote themselves mainly to family law and to the law of property; however, it appears today that they are increasingly interested in company law.

However that may be, the notary cannot ignore taxation. Let us think, for example, of the heavy professional responsibility of the notary with regard to registration taxes. The presence of a tax specialist at a notary's office would be fully justified.

C. Conclusion

Let me draw two conclusions from what I have said so far.

1. The tax consultant fulfils three main functions: the counsel, assistance with deeds and assistance with law disputes. When analysing them, one notices that in the various countries in question, these tasks are not carried out exclusively by tax consultants.

   In those countries where the profession is not organized by law, counsel and assistance with deeds can be given by almost anybody. Even in those countries where the profession is legally organized the tax consultant must share these functions with other professions. As regards assistance and representation in the case of a law suit, one notices two extremes: in France, this function is reserved on the whole for barristers alone, in Germany it also belongs to the realm of the tax consultants. In certain countries the monopoly of the barristers is limited for the benefit of tax consultants.

2. The very absence of a legal organization of the tax consultants' profession in many countries does not encourage the traditional professions, who are moreover subjected to very strict professional codes, to establish interprofessional associations. And yet those who avail themselves of the services of tax consultants would best be served by entities capable of fulfilling each of the tasks listed

above. Furthermore, there are problems that obviously fall within the competence of a number of professionals, and in fact team work appears necessary to solve them.

Thus, whereever the tax consultant's profession has not yet been firmly organized, all conceivable steps must be taken to bring this about, taking into account the three-fold role which the profession is expected to fulfil.

III. Possibility of a lasting professional and interprofessional cooperation

A. Possible forms of cooperation

Professional cooperation can be of many kinds, starting with the mere joining of expenses and ending with the commercial company, not forgetting the intermediate forms such as the private company, with or without juridical personality, and the private professional society in those countries where this type of cooperation is foreseen by the law.

Much depends of the possibilities offered by national legislation and by the orders and associations in the field. The following remarks will show that certain countries have developed appropriate forms of cooperation or are in the process of doing so, while others progress but slowly on the road leading to the team work of the profession in question.

B. Countries where the law has created one or more specific forms of professional societies

1. France

The French legislator is the only one to have created (by the professional law of November 29th, 1966) a specific form of professional society: the "société civile professionnelle". By different decrees, this law has been made applicable to the notaries (1967), auditors (1969), barristers (1972) and legal adivsors (1972). The conditions of application for each of the professions have been determined after consultation of the organizations responsible for the representation of the professions concerned before the public authorities.

The "société civile professionnelle" is a private society which has juridical personality. It is founded by natural persons who practise the same liberal profession and are governed by a legal regimem or whose title is protected. It aims at the common practice of the profession by its members, in spite of the legal provisions which limit the practice of this profession to natural persons.

Unless otherwise stated in the relevant administrative regulation, each associate can become member of only one "société civile professionnelle" and cannot practise the same profession on an individual basis.

Although it is the society that practises the profession, each associate is held personally liable for his professional acts. The society is jointly responsible for any damages caused thereby. The society or the associates must effect a professional risks indemnity in conformity with the relevant administrative regulation.

As regards the management of the society, all the members are to be directors, unless otherwise stated in the statutes, which may designate one or more directors among the associates or provide for their designation by a subsequent decision..

An associate can withdraw from the society either by selling his shares, or by obtaining a refund of his shares from the society. Shares can be transferred or passed on to a third party with the consent of at least three quarters of the associates' voting power, a majority requirement which can be increased by the statutes.

Unless otherwise stated in the relevant administrative regulation, the statutes are to determine the duration of the society. Unless otherwise stated in the same regulation or, failing that, in the statutes, the society is not dissolved following the death, the legal incapacity or the withdrawal, however motivated, of an associate. Neither is it dissolved if one of the associates is hit by a permanent suspension of the right to carry out his profession. If for whatever reason, only one associate remains, he can, within one year, put the situation in order. Should he fail to do so, anybody concerned and in particular the institution which administers the disciplinary jurisdiction can request the society to be dissolved.

Finally, another form of society can be transformed into a "société civile professionnelle" without discontinuance of the existing legal personality.

The "société civile professionnelle" in general permits the creation of pluri-disciplinary groupings. Indeed, art. 2 of the law considers the possibility of societies being established by members of different liberal professions, be these regulated or not. However, the same article stipulates that such a society may perform the acts of a specific profession only through one of its members entitled to practise the profession. Thus, in a society formed among notaries and legal advisors, the latter may not authenticate notarial deeds, since this falls within the exclusive competence of the notary.

It seems, however, that the success of the "société civile professionnelle" is reduced by the fact that it does not really correspond to the needs of partnerships which are of a certain importance, and that it does not offer its members the tax and social security system of wage earners. This is the reason why the legislator has left in doubt the general obligation of practising the profession under the form of a "société civile professionnelle". He has in fact planned to create a new type of professional society subject to the same tax provisions as commercial companies liable either by right or by option to company tax. This innovation has not yet been enacted. In the meantime, legal advisors who until July 1st, 1971, practised their profession through legal entities other than the "société civile professionnelle" (mainly joint stock companies) may continue to do so under certain conditions.

Besides the "société civile professionnelle", law provides for another form of company, the "société civile de moyens". Contrary to the "société civile professionnelle" the "société civile de moyens" does not practise the profession itself, but its aim is to place at its members' disposal all the means which may be useful for the practice of their profession. In this way associates maintain their professional independence and continue to practise their profession individually. The society has no legal links with the professional institutions upon which the associates may depend. I have used the term "may", because the society could have professionals among its members who are subject or not to a legal régime, be they legal entities or natural persons. The society possesses full legal personality, and professionals of different spheres of activity may choose this form of association. In practice, however, it has the same disadvantages following from tax and company law as the "société civile professionnelle".

2. Other countries

Other countries besides France have attempted to organize legally the associate practice of liberal professions. Their efforts have, however, failed.

Thus, in Belgium a bill has been drafted due to the strong

intervention by the "Conseil Supérieur des Classes Moyennes". It provides for the creation of private societies which are very much similar to the French "société civile professionnelle". It is not directed specifically at tax consultants, but it could well apply to interprofessional cooperation in general. Unfortunately, there has been no legislative follow-up to this day.

In Italy, on November 30th, 1977, the Senate adopted a bill moved by Senator A. Vivian, which will probably be submitted in the near future to the vote of the Chamber of Deputies. Its object is the creation of a society among professions of the same or of different disciplines. In general, there may not be more than ten associates. The company will practise the profession. In particular, it will answer for any damage that may occur as a result of the professional activity of its members. The latter shall remain subordinated to the discipline of the orders to which they belong. The other stipulations of the draft bill concern the establishment of the society, its name, the transfer of shares, changes among the personnel, management, the duration and the liquidation. It deals also with the question of incompatibilities.

Finally, in the Federal Republic of Germany, a bill concerning the creation of what might be called the "société civile professionnelle" has been tabled in 1971 (Partnerschaftsgesetz). The bill plans to permit all those practising liberal professions to establish a private company, called "Partnerschaft", having legal personality. Its main characteristics are that of welcoming only as associates those belonging to a professional chamber, be they subjected to different disciplines or not, of declaring the society responsible up to a certain sum total of the possible dammage caused by the professional activity of the associates, who continue to practise at their own risk, and of making obligatory the taking out of a sufficient insurance, which covers the total of its liabilities and which prescribes tax equality for the company in comparison with private companies. This bill has not yet been passed. In the meanwhile, members of the liberal professions can unite together within a company, unless legal or ruling provisions against doing so has been made, as is the case for lawyers and notaries, who may not practise their profession in a company.

C. Countries where the law has not created specific forms of professional societies

In those countries where no specific form of professional company has been created, the option of setting up lasting professional associations depends largely upon the ethical regulations of each of the professions concerned. Let us examine now the content of each of these rules, on the understanding, of course, that it is not possible to go into the details in each country of the various forms under which professional cooperation could be carried out.

1. The Federal Republic of Germany

While waiting for the bill in question to be passed, professional law enables tax consultants, authorized fiscal advisors, chartered accountants, solicitors and notaries in the Federal Republic of Germany to work together either in a common practice or in public companies so as to practise their respective professions together. It even grants the Steuerberater and the Wirtschaftsprüfer the right to carry on their activities in companies with or without a moral personality (Steuerberatungsgesellschaften, Wirtschaftsprüfungsgesellschaften).

The joint office association cannot be given the appearance of a public company, consequently, it cannot be made public.

On the other hand, if it is a public company, the names of the associates must be mentioned in the documents which it publishes. At any rate, the members or associates remain responsible for the professional acts which they draw up. Regarding lawyers and notaries, it has already been stated that they may not unite for the purpose of practising their profession in companies.

Regarding interprofessional cooperation, the pace is set by the Steuerberater. Not only do they permit the establishing of joint practices and of public companies with the Wirtschaftsprüfer, notaries and lawyers, but they also allow the members of the various professions to participate in the administration of the Steuerberatungsgesellschaften which they form among themselves. They agree to this under one condition, that the number of administrators, directors and responsible associates belonging to other professions does not exceed the number of tax consultants. There is in fact no provision which regulated the holding of capital in these types of societies.

The same does not apply to the other professions. According to their professional law the Wirtschaftsprüfer may only have Steuerberater and barristers as associates, to the exclusion of the Steuerbevollmächtigten and of notaries, the barristers only permit Steuerberater and Wirtschaftsprüfer exclude Steuerbevollmächtigte and the notaries, and the notaries can only form an association with lawyers.

At any rate, international professional cooperation is remarkably advanced in the Federal Republic of Germany.

2. The Netherlands

The progress of professional and interprofessional cooperation is yet more remarkable in the Netherlands. Although the legislator has not so far created one more specific forms of professional companies, the orders and professional unions have shown much imagination and have taken many important steps which have considerably improved the professional law in this field. The chartered accountants and the lawyers have been in a position to do this, by virtue of the organizing powers which their orders have by law.

Let us have a look at the situation of the tax consultants, chartered accountants, barristers and notaries, in turn.

a. Tax consultants

The members of the Order of tax consultants can practice their profession either individually or in groups, within public companies, either on a common account or under their joint name with other members of the Order. Recently, they can also practise as a joint stock private partnership (besloten vennootschap), as long as this partnership devotes itself effectively and essentially to tax consulting and that it only has among its shareholders and administrators, members of the Order. Subject to a permission granted by the Council of the Order, members can form a partnership with representatives of other liberal professions, as long as they have had a university education and have to obey the same ethical code as that of the Order. The Order of the barristers is also included in these provisions.

The members of the Fédération of tax consultants, for their part, can practise the profession not only individually or together with other members of the Fédération, but also in the service of these members or of any other physical or moral person approved of by the Council of the Fédération. The following have been approved in this context: the members of the order of tax consultants, recognized chartered accountants, barristers and notaries. Just like the members of the order, the members of the Fédération of tax consultants may practise the profession for a private stock company without being subjected tc regulation regarding the holding of capital and the administration of the company.

Finally, as regards the Brotherhood of tax consultants, this professional union has not yet made its opinion known, on this problem.

b. Chartered Accountants

A recognized chartered accountant, that is to say, a chartered accountant belonging to the Institute (Nederlands Instituut van Registeraccountants) may take up public office either individually or jointly with other independent members of the Institute. The profession of public chartered accountant may also be practised in the form of a private company, limited by shares, or even of a limited company. The statutes must then be approved by the Council of the Institute. This approval is only granted if a certain number of requirements are fulfilled: only recognized chartered accountants can become shareholders, administrators and autitors and they remain responsible for the observance of their ethical code in the work they do in the name of the company.

As regards interprofessional cooperation, the only accepted form is that of a private company and the Council of the Institute must in each case grant permission. The permission can only be granted by the Council if it is established that the independence of the chartered accountant is protected within the association and towards third parties.

It seems, however, that in practice, cooperation with other professions runs into certain difficulties arising either from demands made by the Institute, or lying in the nature of the profession of chartered accountants itself.

Firstly, internal regulations issued by the Institute (Gedragsen beroepsregels registeraccountants) denies chartered accountants the right to make mention of the specific competence of those with whom they have formed limited company. To deny this right runs counter to the conditions laid down by other professionals, such as the barrister and the tax consultant regarding interprofessional cooperation, i. e. to make well known the professional identity of each member.

Furthermore, it has come to notice that services rendered by chartered accountants are by their nature impartial, whereas services rendered by a tax consultant or a barrister are much more partial, this being inherent to the services they render. One might deduce from this, that some of these services and in particular those that consist of assisting and representing parties in the case of law disputes must be held seperate from the more general practices for which the chartered accountant renders services. This point deserves our attention, and shall be taken up later.

c. Barristers

It must be stated that in the Netherlands the barristers are those who show the greatest flexibility in the field of professional and interprofessional cooperation, so much so that the professional law which they have developed can be used as a model in many respects.

In general, the dutch barrister is free to decide in which manner he will cooperate with other lawyers, as long as he takes care to protect his own independence. He may even do so on behalf of a private company limited by shares or of a limited company as long as he continues to observe the ethical code and that shareholders and administrators are all lawyers and that his professional responsability is the same as it would have been, had he practised individually.

The same principles govern cooperation with representatives of other professions. However, interprofessional associations, are only permitted if the associates of the different professions have had a university education or its equivalent, that they belong to an order or to a professional union, whose members are subjected to a discipline comparable to that of the barrister and that the number of the barristers in the internal and external relations of the association be at least equivalent to that of the representatives of the other professions. The Council of the Order decides whether a given profession fulfils the requirements or not. The Council has already cast a favourable judgement regarding the members of the Order of tax consultants and notaries.

The interprofessional association can work under a name which does not necessarily include the names of all the associates. This name need not be altered upon the death, or withdrawal of an associate mentioned therein. Other than that the association must take care that in its external relations, it is clear who is a barrister and who is not.

These last years a number of associations between barristers and notaries have come into existence. They have not yet reached lasting forms of cooperation and are still at the experimental stage.

d. Notaries

A notary can form an association with other notaries as long as his practice remains sufficiently independent with regard to his succession, which is a matter dealt with by the Crown and not by his co-associates. Recently he can also practise in the name of a moral person, which enables him to fall into line with the fiscal statutes of companies.

As regards interprofessional cooperation, the "Confrérie Royale des Notaires" follows the same line of conduct as barristers, which has already been described above.

So, it appears that in the Netherlands, the various professions under study are greatly in favour of interprofessional cooperation. However, regarding the representation of these associations which they favour, they have such diverging requirements that a particular form has to correspond to each individual arrangement, adapted, made to measure, sometimes difficult to find. This is why joint practices are in practice more popular than associations where the names of the participants have to be listed. This fact does not in any way take away from the evidence that in the Netherlands the professions which we have studied are practised more and more in teams and that individual practioners appear increasingly as "rari nantes in gurgite vasto".

3. Ireland and the United Kingdom

In Ireland, the representatives of the liberal professions may not form companies with the intention of practising their profession. On the other hand, partnerships, wherein senior partners devide among themselves the results of the cooperation, while junior partners are remunerated on the basis of a salary are frequent. In these associations the partners are indefinitely responsible for the obligations taken on by the association.

The Irish organizations are opposed to interprofessional associations. At the most they tolerate, for example, that an accountant be employed in a solicitors' firm and vice versa, but they are opposed to his becoming an associate unless he fulfils the requirements of both solicitors and accountants. The Institute of Taxation keeps a close watch over the coordination of the activities of those who are interested in taxation both as accountants and barristers.

In the United Kingdom tax consultants are free to form associations for the practice of their profession, as long as they belong to the Institute of Taxation, the code of ethics of which the latter is gardian remains applicable. Accountants have the right to form companies for all activities other than accountancy itself. Barristers and solicitors may not form such companies.

Interprofessional cooperation runs counter to the corporate spirit of most professions who could take part.

4. Belgium

In Belgium, the liberal professions are slowly moving away from the negative attitude which they had for a long time regarding professional associations. Today, under the pressure of social change they agree to representatives of the same discipline forming a permanent association among themselves. As a general rule they go no further than a public company, as is the case for barristers, notaries and company auditors. Tax consultants and accountants have greater ease since their respective ethical codes are not laid down by virtue of the law.

In the field of interprofessional contacts, individualism and differences existing in professional discipline act as a hindrance regarding the progress of cooperations. Barristers welcome notaries but not tax consultants nor accountants. Company auditors can only form an association with colleagues which adds to the professional endogamy. Notaries are still in doubt as to what they should do.

Just a word on fiduciary companies. As in Switzerland, where their number has greatly increased, fiduciary companies are greatly on the increase in Belgium. They take charge of the organization and control of company accounting and help regarding the administration of tax, social, commercial and industrial law. Their strength resides in the joint practice of a number of professions.

5. Other countries

The examination of the professional and interprofessional contacts in Denmark, Luxembourg and Italy does not allow us to draw other conclusions from the subject. Therefore further investigations will not be carried out at this point.

6. Conclusions

Time has come to draw conclusions from what has been said so far.

1. In general the forming of lasting professional associations among representatives of the same profession does not lead to any major obstacles in the Common Market countries. Some countries have installed a specific form of professional company. Such as France. Others are on the point of doing so. Such as Italy. In those countries where the legislator has abstained so far from taking part, the professionals concerned have shown much imagination.

   There is a greater divergence of opinion as regards the practice of the profession in the form of a commercial company. In the field of tax consulting, only the French and the German legislations recognize this form of professional association. In Belgium and in the Netherlands the Professional Tax Consulting Unions are not opposed to it.

2. In the field of interprofessional cooperation, the situation is not so easy. The main obstacle being the absence of duly harmonized ethical codes. The example of the French "société civile professionnelle" shows that the most important factor is not, that the professions be regulated by law or by virtue of the law. The important thing is that they be regulated by sufficiently equivalent disciplinary rules for a lasting interprofessional association to take shape.

   In this line of thought, it seems that a lasting interprofessional association should take all three as models. The French "société civile professionnelle", the German "Partnerschaftsgesetz", as well as the pattern adopted by the Dutch barristers. On the basis of the various principles found therein one could imagine a company - commercial or public - whose characteristics would be the following:

- the company would have moral personality;
- it could be formed only among professionals who have had a University education or its equivalent and who belonged to comparable disciplinary systems. It could only be established if the professional independence of each associate was sufficiently ensured;
- the nominal capital and administration of the company would be in the hands of the associates alone. Each profession would have its share in the internal and external relations of the company;
- the associates would remain individually bound by the disciplinary law of their own profession;
- acts which by their nature belonged to one particular profession could not be carried out by anyone other than a member of that profession (e. g. notary deeds should be drawn up by notaries);
- associates would remain personally responsible for the professional acts they accomplish. The company would carry responsability only up to a certain amount. The company would cover the responsability it assumed by taking out an insurance policy;
- the company could work under a name which included the name of at least one of the associates (professional). The name would remain in the ownership of the company even if an associate whose name is used has resigned or had died;
- documents established under the trade name of the company would not need to bear the names of all the associates. The signature of the associates dealing with the matter would be sufficient.

If this specific form of company could also enable associates to fall into line with the fiscal and social status of companies, it seems a major step forward would have been accomplished towards a lasting interprofessional association.

IV. Possibilities of lasting professional and international cooperation beyond frontiers

To bring about the social and economic integration objectives which it had set itself, the Treaty of Rome prescribes the free movement of goods, persons, services and capital. We are mainly concerned here with the liberalization of the right of establishment and of the provision of services. The mutual recognition of qualifications adds to the problem.

A. Right of establishment and rendering of services

Regarding the right of establishment the European Commission has drafted various propositions for Directive aiming at the elimination of discrimination based exclusively on nationality. These propositions which also concern tax consultants and accountants have become superfluous and have consequently been withdrawn following Reyners judgement pronounced on June 21st, 1974 by the Court of Justice in Luxembourg.

Reyners was of Dutch nationality and held the legal diploma necessary in Belgium to become barrister-at-law. The question was whether he could be refused access to this profession in Belgium on the grounds of his nationality, since Belgian law stipulates that Belgian nationality is necessary in order to be called to the bar.

The Court of Justice decided that he could not be refused access to the bar, since all discriminations based on nationality are contrary to the provisions of the Treaty. The member States must thus apply the principle of equal treatment for all professions, even if this has not been regulated by a directive. On the other hand, the Van Binsbergen decree pronounced on December 3rd, 1974 by the Court of Luxembourg, has shown that no Member State can keep a national from another Member State from rendering services free from all limitations.

Van Binsbergen was a Dutch national who was represented in the Court of his country by a Dutch legal advisor. In these courts the profession of the barrister is free, only persons residing in the Netherlands, however, can act as mandates. During the proceedings the legal advisor had his residence transfered to Belgium. The disputed question was whether he could continue pleading in the Dutch Courts.

The Court of Justice decided that this was lawful, on the grounds that decisions taken by a Member State with the intention of denying persons established in another Member State, the right to provide services and which is not subject to any special condition under the national law applicable, are contrary to the provisions of the Treaty. The Court added that a requirement of habitual residence could not be imposed on this professional since this in effect would make impossible the rendering of services. In such a case the choice of a domicile would suffice.

This does not mean that the host country cannot take lawful measures so as to restrict the provision of services in certain cases. The Van Binsbergen judgement does not consider "specific requirements imposed on the person to be incompatible with the Treaty where they have as their purpose the application of professional rules justified by the general good - in particular rules relating to organisation, qualifications, professional ethics, supervision and liability - which are binding upon any person established in the State in which the service is provided, where the person providing the service would escape from the ambit of those rules by being established in another Member State." Nor is it incompatible with the Treaty, for a Member

State to take special measures "to prevent the exercise by a person providing services whose activity is entirely or principally directed towards its territory, for the purpose of avoiding the professional rules of conduct which would be applicable to him if he were established within that State; such a situation may be subject to judicial control under the provisions of the chapter relating to the right of establishment and not of that on the provision of services."

The harmonization of the various professional regimes become all the more urgent. In this regard the Council Directive of March 22, 1977 to facilitate the effective exercise by lawyers of freedom to provide services, deserves particular attention. According to that directive, any advocate coming from one of the eight other countries may appear in Court to defend a client or before the public authorities under the same conditions as those provided for advocates in the host Member State, without there being a requirement of habitual residence in that country and without having to enroll with the competent professional organization in the country of practice. He must, however, observe the professional rules of the host-country, while at the same time continuing to observe those of the country of origine (principle of double ethics). Each Member State can require that he be introduced to the presiding judge or that he work in conjunction with a lawyer who practises before the judicial authority in question. The regulations concerning the provision of services outside the courts are less strict.

But it is not necessary to wait for the publishing of a Community Directive in order to contribute anything to professional cooperation on a transnational basis. The advocates had proven this well before the Directive of March 22, 1977. Already in 1973 the consulting Commission of the European Community Bar had established a model convention among bars as a means of liberating the provision of services. Under the auspices of that same Commission, two conventions of professional reciprocity have been signed between the bar in Paris on the one hand, and two Anglo-Saxon professional associations on the other: The Senate of the Inns of Court and the bar (19th December 1975), and the Law Society of England and Wales (12th April 1976). These conventions aim at regulating the establishment of Parisian advocates in the United Kingdom and that of the solicitors and barristers in Paris. They authorize the formation of joint practices and give their support to the principle of double ethics.

B. Diplomas

The liberalization of the right of establishment and of the rendering of services depends greatly of the mutual recognition of diplomas necessary for the practice of the profession. The recognition of qualifications as equivalents for these titles is one of the main goals. Indeed, the elimination of discriminating measures and the harmonization of legal provisions and regulations would remain a "dead letter", if the profession could not be practised in the host country on the grounds of the latter refusing to recognize the equivalence of diplomas delivered by the country of origin.

The Thieffry judgement, delivered on April 28th, 1977 by the Court of Justice stated that a distinction must be made between two different categories: on the one hand between university recognitions, granted with a view to permitting the pursuit of certain studies, and a recognition having "civil effect", granted with a view to permitting the pursuit of a professional activity. The Court put forward the principle that a national legislation which provides for recognition of equivalence only for university purposes does not of itself justify the refusal to recognize such equivalence as evidence of a professional qualification. The act of demanding the national diploma prescribed by the legislation of the country of establishment constitutes, even in the absence of the directives provided for, a restriction incompatible with the freedom of establishment guaranteed by the Treaty. This is an important conclusion whose far reaching importance will not fail to be noted by anyone.

Nearer to us, the proposal for a Directive concerning the approval of persons in charge of the legal control of accounts, of joint stock companies. It was submitted to the Council by the Commission on April 24th, 1978.

This Proposal for a Directive does not state anything on the question of diplomas. It merely prescribes that a natural person can only be entitled to practise the activities of the profession after having reached the standard necessary for university entry followed by a higher education and passed an examination of professional aptitude of university level or its equivalent, organized or recognized by the State.

It authorizes the Member States to acknowledge foreign nationals, under condition that they have obtained the qualifications outside the host country which the competent authorities consider objectively equivalent to those made necessary by the Directive. It should be noted that the qualifications held by a person from another State, must at any rate be considered equivalent if approval has already been granted in that State, in application of the Directive.

It should also be noted that approval can be granted under certain conditions to moral persons or other kinds of societies or professional associations. On the basis of this provision, the proposition makes the various forms of structure under which the profession is practised, law.

In effect, the proposal for a directive enables Member States to approve of all persons who fulfil the conditions it imposes.

It is not concerned so much with the practice of a profession, as with the carrying out of a task: the legal control of annual accounts of joint stock companies. Certain countries leave this task up to a number of professions while others include it in the tasks of one specific company.

Nevertheless one might fear that the Directive will fail in its aim each time the legal control of the profession is regulated by legislative provisions and regulations which are restrictive. In Belgium, legal control is up to the members of the Institute of company directors alone. Must the foreign professional who whishes to practise in Belgium then become a company auditor and member of the Institute? At any rate he may not form an association for the purpose of practising his profession with one or more company auditors as long as he has not become himself a member of the Institute, because the law forbids company auditors to form an association with persons who have not themselves this qualification. And even if he were a member of the Institute his association with a colleague would necessarily be limited to that of a public company, because the law stipulates that an association formed in such a way may not have the same form as a limited company.

It is obvious that such stipulations hinder international professional and interprofessional associations, despite the urgency which is felt in that regard.

V. General Conclusions

The use of professional and interprofessional associations, both national and international, in the field of tax consulting need, it is hoped, no longer be stressed. This point has been made and stressed in the introduction to this study.

The difficulties one meets with to bring these about are not insurmountable. They are essentially of three kinds: those concerning prohibitive internal clauses, those concerning the respective ethical codes and those coming from the nature itself of the professions in question.

When legislative provisions and/or regulations hinder the freedom of association either among persons belonging to different liberal professions, or among persons belonging to the same liberal profession, it is advisable to abolish these hindrances by legislative means and/or regulations which brought them about. The example given by the bar of Paris and of the United Kingdom demonstrate that Community Directives are not essential to the realization of cooperation, even beyond frontiers.

Certain liberal professions are organized by law, others are not. The fact that a liberal profession cannot make good of the will of the legislator for its organization does in no way take away from the right to exist of the professional and interprofessional associations which that profession intends to establish, or with which it intends to participate. The Dutch example proves this point. Independence must be ensured for each participating profession, within interprofessional associations. The organizations of these professions presupposes a uniformisation of the codes of Ethic.

Finally, the very nature of these professions which social trends tend to combine must be taken into account. Even if it is true, that some of them are more dedicated than others, which might be considered at first impartial, it remains nonetheless that their cooperation is an established fact and that each one has its own particular task to carry out. May we quote as a conclusion to our study the words of the President of the French Bar, Albert Brunois, Member of the Institute, President of the Advisory Committee of the European Community Bar: In each country, professional practice is linked to certain servitudes which will no doubt have to disappear, in accordance with the liberating policy which the authors of the Treaty of Rome had in mind; this liberalization must obey certain transcendental normes, bringing about a creative synthesis of the uniforming European spirit and of the legislative and strictly professional realities, which are in force in each State.

Discussion

Mr. Möckershoff, Steuerberater, President of the Bundessteuerberaterkammer (Germany)

We have discussed cooperation as it exists, in particular in Germany, among the professional groups in question, the tax consultants, the chartered accountants and the solicitors. A remarkable factor in Germany, in comparison to the other countries, is that each of these three professional groups have clear legal regulations: We have a law for tax consulting, we have an order of Chartered Accountants and we also have the Federal solicitors' order. The training and examinations which are necessary to practise these professions have been clearly defined. These laws also define clearly the respective tasks which these professional groups have to carry out. The tarifs in application are also prescribed and finally a professional control is also organized. Professional or special tax courts keep a watch over the observance of professional regulations. I mention this because certain problems arise as a consequence of these legal regulations. It is not so, that there are no problems at all in Germany because of these laws.

In this way, the Rechtsanwalt (solicitor) can act as a tax consultant in all fields, of course also in the field of legal advising. The only exception in these three groups resides in particular in the fact that he may not sign certificates, which the chartered accountants may do. The position of the chartered accountant is similar. He is free to practise tax consulting in all fields. He is only limited in comparison to the solicitor (Rechtsanwalt) in his rights as a legal advisor. But he may, just like the tax consultant (Steuerberater) appear in court in the appropriate fields. In third place, is the tax consultant in Germany who, it is true, just like the chartered accountant (Wirtschaftsprüfer) may not act as a legal advisor in an unlimited way, and who furthermore cannot draw up certificates.

A further remark on Prof. Couturier's paper: He spoke of companies. From our point of view, I would like to underline that we can practise in the large sense, in the form of partnerships, of joint stock companies, of public companies and limited companies and these three professional groups can practise their professions together in these companies under certain conditions. I must underline however that these possibilities are in fact only open to Steuerberater (tax consultants) and Wirtschaftsprüfer (chartered accountants). The Rechtsanwalt (solicitor) may not practise his profession in Germany under the form of a joint stock company, that is neither in a limited company, nor in a limited partnership. On the other hand he may practise his profession through a tax consulting company and even possibly through a chartered accounting company.

At the moment - at least in the field of tax consulting - we are firmly decided to prevent abuses with regard to tax consulting companies. We are trying to get new laws enacted, with this aim in view. The following problems arise, namely in Germany:

For example, these above mentioned companies can be formed by persons who do not belong to the profession. That is to say, these partnerships (partnerships limited by shares) and these limited companies can be formed by persons who are neither Wirtschaftsprüfer (chartered accountants) nor Steuerberater (tax consultants) nor Anwälte (solicitors). The companies can thus be in the hands of persons who do not belong to the profession. So far the only regulations which exists is that - for example, in the case of a tax consulting company - at least one of the members of the board of directors must be a tax consultant. The other members of the board of directors can be either chartered accountants or solicitors or even other persons. But there are certainly possibilities of abuse at the shareholders' level. We have the firm intention of bringing about a change here. As far as I can see the chartered accountants also have the same intention. The number of such companies is very much on the increase in Germany. At the moment there are, nevertheless, about 1000 tax consulting companies and about 600 chartered accounting companies. We expect that the legislator - and we will try apply as much pressure as possible - will put an end to the forming of companies by persons other than members of the profession, for example professional organizations and economic groups.

Further problems reside in the representation of companies; opinions differ in this regard. You know that the Anwälte (solicitors) in Germany may only carry out their profession in the form of companies, and the profession of solicitors in Germany has no intention that legal advice be given in the form of joint stock companies. I would just like to add that in this field all concerned feel that this kind of joint stock company as it exists in our country is not necessarily the best possible solution and that we have been trying for many years to find a special kind of company form, for the liberal professions. The so-called "Partnerschaftsgesetz" has unfortunately not been adopted yet, after two legislative periods. I have noted, however, that we in the "Bundesverband der freien Berufe" (The Federal Association of the Liberal Professions) have been trying to prepare a new "Partnerschaftsgesetz" and to include it in the legal procedure. The "Partnerschaftsgesetz" has the advantage that this form of company is adapted in particular to the liberal professions, unlike the joint stock company, as has been mentioned above, which gives rise to a series of problems.

There are also specific professional problems of taxation in Germany since, of course, different taxation is applied to individual persons, private companies and joint stock companies. Other problems are related to the name and the liability. Particular problems which exist despite legal provisions can be dealt with during the further course of the discussion.

Dr. Stefano Bertorello (Italy)

I would first of all like to apologize for anything I might repeat which Prof. Couturier has already said about Italy. But I hope to be able to add something new.

According to Italian law, the tax payer may only be advised and/or represented in court by persons belonging to specific liberal professions, i. e. by persons who are on the barristers' or notaries' register, by "dottori commercialisti" (they are qualified economists), by "ragioneri" (they are chartered accountants), by architects, geometricians, certified agricultural experts, engineers, technicians, agricultural engineers and by qualified persons belonging to other occupations. Furthermore, an Italian law dating back to 1958 grants retired civil servants of the Finance Ministry, who have been enrolled on a special register kept by the Italian Finance Ministry, the right to assist and represent parties in court in matters of taxation.

At the moment university professors in the field of tax law

or economics, and who are not enrolled on any register, are paradoxically excluded from tax consulting. The same applies to qualified persons from specialized faculties, for whom there is no professional association, so, for example for social and political scientists, statisticians or other specialized professional groups, even if they, by the very nature of their work have knowledge in the field of taxation, which is so tightly linked to economic and social life. It is evident to-day that the absurd exclusion of these professional groups must be lifted with view of their scientific or even general education. So as to help in this direction a draft has been submitted by a member of Parliament to the Italian Parliament in January of this year, which plans the organization of tax associations in each of the provinces of our Republic. This draft is far from being perfect, and needs to be discussed and completed. However, when it becomes national law, which is certain, the consequence will be the official institutionalization of a new profession in Italy, namely that of the profession of the tax consultant, which is to this day excluded from the Italian order. Indeed, Italy is one of six member states of the European Communities, in which there is no recognized autonomous profession of the tax consultant.

In my opinion, and I am now speaking personally, it is important in the context of the final resolution, Mr. President, that an urgent and official request be made to the Italian Parliament and to the departments of the governments concerned, so that the above mentioned draft be not buried. The law must enter into force, a law which would correspond to the example of the French or of the German, and if you like of the Belgian law, and must regulate the following aspects:

1. It must ensure that counsel and/or representation in court be carried out exclusively by highly qualified persons, belonging to one of the traditional professional associations

we have today. I have the aforementioned "dottori commercialisti" and "ragioneri" in mind.

2. Other persons must be entitled to carry out tax consulting on the grounds of their experience in the field of taxation, or of other factors, or of their knowledge, even if they are not enrolled on the professional register mentioned above.
3. The need to keep the standard of the technical and legal education as high as possible, must be stressed, because these play a very important role for the enterprises.

   I hope that I can say this in the name of all those present and for all the members of the European Communities.

Prof. Dr. Albert Tiberghien, President of the C.F.E. (Belgium)

I would like to thank Mr. Bertorello for his contribution. I would also like to add the following as regards procedure. The Confédération Fiscale Européenne does not intervene automatically with the national governments, but upon a request made by its members, the Confédération can intervene with a national government. That is to say, if the "associatione nationale des tributaristi italiani" which is a member of the Confédération and which is represented by four administrators on the Administrative Board supports your request, we shall intervene with your government.

Mr. John W. Smith, chartered accountant (Great Britain)

I hope that it might perhaps interest our friends in Europe to learn a little of how the giving of tax advice, in practice happens in Great Britain.

It should be borne in mind that most businesses in Britain even relatively small ones, are conducted in the form of a limited company, which must by law have a professional audit conducted each year. Thus the Institute of Chartered Accountants and, a somewhat smaller body, the Association of Certified Accountants have grown quite large in the auditing of businesses and they now virtually have a monopoly in this field. Out of this has developed the giving of day-by-day tax advice to the companies which the Chartered and Certified Accountants audit and nearly all day-by-day tax advice in Britain is given by firms of chartered accountants. The partners in these firms begin their training by doing largely accounting work but if they become particularly interested, they gradually specialize in tax work and often complete their education in this field by studying for the examinations of the Institute of Taxation. The Members of the Institute of Chartered Accountants and the Association of Certified Accountants may appear in the lowest tax courts in Britain on behalf of tax payers, but when an appeal either to the lower law court, when it appears to be a matter of great substance, or where it is clear that the case is going to go to a High Court then a solicitor is always brought in to act alongside the accountant at a fairly early stage in the negociations. There are in fact relatively few firms of solicitors that specialize in tax work.

If the matter is going to go to a very high court the preparation of the appeal will be conducted by a solicitor, the actual presentation of the case in court will be the work of a barrister. In addition to tax appeals the larger firms of solicitors also find themselves giving considerable tax advice in connection with the contracts for, for example, the buying and selling of businesses or the entering into very important and commercial transactions.

General Debate

Prof. Dr. Albert Tiberghien, President of the C.F.E. (Belgium)

I would first of all like to greet, Mr. Heisel, Directeur des Impôts, who is here on behalf of the French Minister for Finance.

Also I am glad to tell you that Mr. Couturier, who was to be this morning's rapporteur, has arrived in Brussels from Rouanda at 6.30 AM. He came over to Strasbourg as quickly as possible so as to be present at least for our discussion. I shall ask him to take the floor in a few minutes.

I would now like to call on Mr. Lecce for a short statement. May I thank Mr. Lecce for the interesting brochure he has written and made available to us.

Dott. Salvatore Lecce (Italy)

Before I get to the point, may I first of all extend my thanks to the organizing committee of this Congress, on behalf of Italy, which I have the honour of representing here and I think I am speaking on behalf of all those present, if I ask you to accept our warmest congratulations for this very successful Congress for which you, Mr. President, Mr. Vice-President, have been responsible as well as our dear Secretary General, Mr. Gerhard, who went to a great deal of trouble for the success of this Congress and who deserves our warmest congratulations. I would also like to congratulate my dear colleague, Professor Croxatto, who is representing here our friend Delattre, to whom we sent yesterday a get well telegramme on behalf of the Congress.

I would like to make a suggestion. The force and vitality of our Confédération Fiscale Européenne has been put to evidence, and I would like to make a proposition on behalf of Italy, that is, that the next Congress be held in Italy, and we are honoured to be able to ask you to come to our country, to organize something which I hope would not be less good than that which our friend, Mr. Gerhard, has been able to provide. Thank you, Mr. President, for having accepted our suggestion.

To get back to what I wanted to say, I would like to remind you all that the science of finances is a branch of economic policy. Adam Smith has dealt with the problems of the science of finances (i. e. taxation and public finance) in his monumental work "Inquiry into the Nature and Causes of the Wealth of Nations". And what is the meaning of this? It means that the science of finance must be manoeuvered within the limits of economic laws. If our financial legislation does not go along with economic laws, we are not taking good financial decisions. We end up by destroying the source of income and what really represents the wealth, not only of European nations, but of the whole world. So, taking it from this principle, may I submit to this highly qualified Congress the need to consider taxation from the point of view of economic laws, that is to recognize that certain principles, such as the equality of the tax burden of John Stuart Mill, based on the decrease of the marginal utility of income be well examined, because the increasing rate of taxes in the end destroys the source of income itself. We are now in a situation in Italy, for example, where one can really ask oneself why one is working. In the long run the contractors are left with nothing. They say to themselves: I work from morning to night but I am no longer boss in my own company. I am forced to ask myself what am I doing, where all this is taking us.

We must ask ourselves the question, whether we want a free Europe, a democrat , Europe, a Europe with a liberal economy, moderated by interventions so as to avoid anarchy taking over our liberties; if we want this we must look at economic laws and interprete finances in a liberal way. If, on the other hand, we want a society of slaves, you can be assured, I won't have anything else to add. I think we want a free Europe for our sons. I recalled that a United Europe signifies a great force, a force that will give prestige to our continent. A divided and weak Europe has no significance, we will no longer have any faith in the future destiny of humanity.

We must understand this situation. I am speaking out of the great love I have for the whole of Europe. I make no distinctions of nationalities. "Si vis pacem para bellum", reads an antique latin proverb, if we want peace, let us be strong. If we are weak our continent will become a colony exploited by other continents. It is for this reason, I have written this little brochure, so as to recall these principles to all, these feelings that must guide us in the forming of a new Europe. We shall have to have two homelands, our original homeland and our larger homeland, called Europe. If we do not see things in this light, we shall no longer be of any significance for the destinies of humanity.

This is why I want to tell you that we must diminish tax pressures in all the countries of the Community. It is necessary that the progression of the tax rates be considerably decreased. The same applies to value added tax rates. We have, for example, made a great difference between products of first necessity, and other luxury products. I think that all these products are simply industrial and commercial goods, and that none of these products should be either advantaged or disadvantaged such as is the case in Italy with luxury goods which are taxed at a 35 % rate, this can destroy a company's chance and must be stopped.

I have written all I wanted to say on this in the little brochure which I had the honour of making available for you, and I hope you will have the time to have a little look at it and to think on the propositions I have made and to let your voices be heard at this Congress so as to tell the Authorities of the European Communities what are the fundamental lines it should follow, so that we may have a free Europe, an independ Europe, a Europe which has once again the force and power of its commercial and industrial energy and which has been able to spread civilization and which we do not want to see crushed like a little colony which would be exploited by other continents.

Prof. Dr. Albert Tiberghien, President of the C.F.E. (Belgium)

May I thank Count Lecce for his brilliant contribution. It is, indeed a good thing that we all consider ourselves technicians and mechanics of taxation, that we guide ourselves along the lines of grand human principles, the principles of European unity, which command our lives today and which should guide also our daily fiscal operations. Our thanks once again.
I thank in particular Mr. Lecce, because it is he who first had the idea of this congress. He made the suggestion long

ago, at a meeting of our Administrative Board, too soon, of course, it was then not yet possible to hold such a congress, but it was Count Lecce who I always had in mind when we discussed the possibility of holding this Congress.

Mr. Alain Tinayre, avocat, President of the "Union Nationale des Associations des Professions Libérales" (UNAPL), (France)

I thank you, Mr. President, for giving me the floor for a few moments, so that I may convey to you the message of friendship and of brotherhood of the "Union Nationale des Associations des Professions Libérales Francaises". The French liberal professions have during the last few months grouped together and experienced a kind of awakening so as to undertake action of a trade union kind, with the intention of winning back, both in the eyes of the public authorities and in those of the French public, their true image and the real position which this professional sector holds. You understand, of course, that in this attempt and in that action, your activities and the professional branch you represent is very much in the foreground of our thoughts. I must say that it was with the greatest interest that I heard all the preceding speakers and that I was able to mesure to what extent the spirit, the research, and the sense of belonging to a liberal profession was for you of the utmost importance. This not only for the French tax consultants, a fact, I was already aware of, but also for European tax consultants, which I was less conscious of. I must add that we felt that at a time and in a world where the citizen is at the mercy of increasingly powerful economic and technocratic forces, it has become ever so valuable and more valuable than ever, be it in the medical world, the legal or in the technical world, to have a counsel capable of establishing a personal contact, which one is free to choose, who is responsible and above all who is independent. It is because of all these various criterias, which seem to us to be essential, not so much for those who practise the profession, as for those who avail of its services, and for those for whom it is there, that the "Union des Professions Libérales Françaises" undertook this action and that it finds all the interest I have just told you about, concerning your work.

If I were to give you a message on behalf of the "Union des Professions Libérales Françaises", at this stage of your work, I would say that I am particularly interested by the research which you are doing on your status, and that I am not unaware of all the difficulties your research has to contend with. But among the most precious goods which need to be protected regarding the establishing of a status for an activity such as yours, it seems to me that the most precious factor is that of independence. It is important while practising an activity such as yours that you should practise it freely, and in all independence and if I may say so, free of the forces and dangers which in your branch are almost more important than for the other liberal professions, I mean the economic danger and the capitalist danger, and if I may add the technocratic danger. In your field more than in any other, the tax consultant is in danger of finding himself under the influence of strong economic forces. He may run the risk of being under the power of a strong administrative force. Both these dangers must be avoided. It is thanks to the status of a liberal professional, that you will be able to avoid them and this is why I feel today, and I have the backing of the Union des Professions Libérales on this, so close to you and to the research you are doing. Thank you for not forgetting the indepence of our professions, thank you for the work you are doing.

Please accept the message of friendship of the liberal professions which I represent, and which in this country of France are experiencing a rebirth and finding once more their true dimension.

Dr. Ulrich Zuschke, EC-Commission

I represent the department in the Commission in Brussels, which works on questions regarding the freedom of movement of the liberal professions. In that sense I am here today, among you as your guest and as such I am not really entitled to make a statement on your draft resolution. But with view of the long and confident collaboration which connects us, I have the courage to do, what otherwise would have seemed incorrect; I feel all the more promted to speak in that I am particularly concerned with the part of your resolution which deals with freedom of movement.

The principles contained in your draft resolution are excellent and they represent all our objectives. However, in the way they are ordered and phrased here, they contain perhaps a slight danger, which could be avoided. And it is on this point that I would like to say a few words, as an outsider.

What I mean with this perhaps slightly mysterious introduction will become clearer once we have taken a look at the situation as it appears to-day in the field of the professional freedom of movement of the tax consulting profession. In that respect, I can first of all refer to two points which came to light very well during Prof. Couturier's profound and detailed paper: The present situation is first of all marked by the disappearance of limitations in all national legislations, which restricts the practice of a profession to the nationals of that state. We now have the so-called "inland treatment", i. e.

a Member State, for example the Federal Republic of Germany, may not treat a member of the profession from another State, lets say from France, differently and may not exclude him from a professional activity on the grounds that he is not German.

Just how this "inland treatment" works out, depends on a further point which Prof. Couturier also stated clearly, namely: Is the activity in the member State in question reglemented or is it free? If it is free then the Italian in France, the Irishman in Denmark can practise the profession just like any of the nationals of the country in question. If it is not free, if it is subject to certain regulations, then equal treatment of foreigners and nationals means that one expects of the foreigner all the qualifications one expects of the national, this means in particular that one expects that he have had the same training.

This in fact means - applied to the field of freedom of movement for the tax consulting profession - the following: We have in Germany - as we have heard - very detailed regulations concerning the activity and the title. Not only is it impossible to use the title, if one has not had a specific training, but one may not practise the profession if one has not had the education in question. In other States, in France the use of the title is subject to certain regulations, in Italy - and that was very well put in evidence in Dr. Bertorello's contribution - there is also a set of rules. In Italy one cannot practise the profession freely although the monopoly is fairly extensive in its application. The consequences are as follows: The German "Steuerberater" can practise the profession everywhere, where there is no regulation, the other nationals only have the possibility of practising their profession in Germany if they have gone to the effort of doing their studies in Germany and of passing the Steuerberater examination. The "inland treatment" and this is what I would like to stress in this context, gives a foreigner the possibility of sitting for the Steuerberater examination. The limitations which existed in the old version of the Steuerberater laws have been changed according to the jurisdiction of the Court of Justice.

There is not a 100 % freedom of movement, because we have States in which the profession is regulated and some where it is not. So as to bring about a complete freedom of movement, one must think of the possibilities of using the qualifications from the country of origin in the new country, the treaty of Rome contains regulations on this point - that is Article 57, which foresees so as to alleviate the practice of certain professions that the diploma in question be mutually recognized. If the education is very different, then it is evident that a recognition of qualifications cannot always be granted, and that the education itself must first of all be comparable. The recognition of qualifications can be made on this basis. The difficulty lies in the great difference between the Member States, for it is not possible in the near future, to make the education similar, and on the other hand one is up against very detailed regulations in some cases and the absence of any kind of regulation in others. It is for this reason that the Commission suggested a very humble solution as a mesure of transition, which aims at a situation where the diploma, as it applies in the Member States concerned, coupled with four years practical experience should be recognized in all the other Member States. This solution has given rise to concern among the German members of the profession, namely that persons who have not had the thorough education which the Steuerberater has had, can come to Germany and enjoy the same rights as the German Steuerberater.

I think that this fear is too pessimistic, and indeed for two reasons. First of all it is not true that the measures of transition which were planned by the Commission, grant all rights. There is a very important difference between this measure of transition and a full mutual recognition. It only grants the right to use the title of the country of origin. This means that on the basis of this regulation the French person who wishes to act as a tax consultant in Germany may not on the basis of this directive call himself a "Steuerberater", he must call himself "conseil fiscal". There is thus still a considerable difference between that and a complete mutual recognition.

According to experience made so far, a complete freedom of movement does not automatically lead to great moves. Indeed today although the profession is not regulated in other countries and on the contrary it is free, a considerable number of Germans do not leave for other member states, on the contrary, despite the four years of application of the "inland treatment" there has not been much change. Above all moves in one direction alone have not been noted.

We have been able to gather some experience in the field of freedom of movement in connection with the freedom of movement of doctors. As you probably know, the directive concerning the recognition of the doctor's diplomas has become effective since December 1976. Before then, there had been both hopes and fears. One had feared that States on the grounds that the organization of their health service would not have been very attractive for doctors, would not have experienced much movement, while States where the conditions of practice of the medical profession are attractive, would have been overrun. Nothing of the like has happened. Many doctors have come to the apparently unattractive States from other Member States and the countries which had feared to be overrun by great numbers because of their attractive conditions of practice, found that this did not happen. One can say, - I do not have the exact figures here -, that the situation about balances. That is why I do not think it should be feared that the introduction of the freedom of movement in the field of tax consulting would lead to a disbalance with a greater amount of movement in one direction.

Now to get back to the draft resolution: as I said, the principles which it contains are, taken individually, perfect. If, as is stated in para. b. in the draft resolution, the rendering of services across frontiers is only brought about once the harmonization of the law of the profession has been brought about, then we should be aware of the fact that the free rendering of services across froniers will be delayed for a long time yet and this is certainly not the intention of all concerned. We shall not be able to bring about harmonization, - which of course has to be done and which must remain a long term objective of European integration -, quickly enough so as to be able to introduce in good time a full freedom of the rendering of services. If I may make the following humble suggestion, as an outsider, I would say under b) that the words "after the harmonization of the law of the profession" should be left out.

Prof. Dr. Albert Tiberghien, President of the C.F.E. (Belgium)

When we demand that the laws and obligations of our profession in the European Communities be established according to uniform principles, this demand is not directed at the Commission, but at the individual States and also at ourselves. We should not wait that the legal regulation be carried out in each State so as to arrive at a liberalization. As regards liberalization, we stated in our notice of April 21st, 1977 a demand not for a transitory measure, but a direct and definit regulation.

Mr. Winfried Wachter, Steuerberater (Germany)

Yesterday's discussion of Mr. Hofstra's paper has not yet been included in the draft resolution on page 2, last paragraph, but only the paper itself. For this reason, I would like to suggest that the last paragraph on page 2, which is on the net wealth tax be formulated in the following way: The effect of net wealth tax should not be seen in isolation but within the general context of the taxes levied on capital by that state or by other entities as e.g. inheritance and gift tax, tax on land and buildings etc. On the grounds of the practical experience made to date, the introduction of a net wealth tax should be avoided, because of its disadvantages in particular with regard to the harmonization of the conditions of competition, and as the case may be, it should be eliminated.

Mr. Karl Krammig, Steuerberater (Germany)

I would like to ask a fundamental question regarding the first part of this final communiqué: it seems to be suggested in the second paragraph, that the Treaty of Rome contains a request made to the Commission, or the case may be, to the Counsel of Ministers, that tax law should be harmonized on incomes and wealth and returns. The Roman Treaties say nothing on this. It is only stated in the Treaty of Rome that customs and consumer taxes should be harmonized. The reason being, that these taxes are put on goods in a visible way, and as a result they could be done away with or harmonized as the case may be. Income tax and tax on wealth and similar taxes - this has been disputed in the past, but this is no longer the case - are included in the price of the goods. It is no longer possible to calculate just how high this tax percentage is.

For this reason, it is the responsibility of the national legislative authority to see that distortions in competition, which are caused by unequal taxation be eliminated in each country. If they do not do this, the European Communities cannot do it for them. This is the real meaning of this regulation in the Roman Treaty

If this is so, just as I have described it, then in my opinion, it is not at all our responsibility as a European Union of tax consultants to see that the Commission bring about a harmonization.

The national professional associations of this Confédération should rather turn to their national Parliaments, so that they can create a situation, which will not create distortions in competition.

Prof. Dr. Horst Vogel, Steuerberater und Rechtsanwalt (Germany)

It is the task of the Commission to set down data also in the field of commercial law and in the field of direct taxes, in the context of a general growth policy. The Commission has already attempted during the 60s to work out uniform principles, or at least harmonized principles. We would be taking a step backwards, if we were to, - pardon me, Mr. Krammig - make even an appeal to the national legislative authorities. It is the task of the Commission to set up a uniformed market, both in the field of direct and indirect taxes. A uniformed market can only be set up if in the field of direct and indirect taxes, for which the methods of calculation are still absolutely uncertain, uniform and harmonized regulations exist. For this reason, I fully adhere to the tenor of the resolution.

I would just like to make a small remark: on page 2, in the

paragraph which reads ..." a common solution to the problem of the relationship between commercial and tax accounting" ... it would be wise to add ... "on the basis of the 4th directive, since we have one dating which dates back to last July. This, in my view, would underline the importance of the 4th directive.

We can consider ourselves fortunate, that we already have got a directive on commercial law. Regarding wealth tax, I share Mr. Wachter's idea. We should not elaborate on the wording during this discussion. That is the task of the Committee in charge of the resolution, our President and his collaborators. The idea should be voiced that special care be given to the burden caused by wealth tax, in particular on the propensity and capacity of investment.

Mr. Raymond Heisel, Directeur Régional des Impôts (France)

If your work is to have a tangible outcome you must first of all be realistic. However, I feel, for my part, that the harmonization of taxes which you have requested in paragraph 3 of your draft resolution should be preceeded by the harmonization of taxes on incomes and profits. But this is not going to happen overnight, as you all know. On the other hand, just as you request in the first paragraph of page 2, it should be possible to introduce within a reasonable delay a common solution to income and profit determination, which while waiting for an even better solution, could be altered up or down to meet specific national accounting, so that they might be better adapted to the taxation of each country. We would thus at least, have a common system which at any rate, is a first step.

Dr. Fritz Eggesiecker, Steuerberater (Germany)

We heard this morning Mr. Couturier's excellent paper which was held in an inimitable way. I now have the draft resolution in my hand, and I notice the absence of a considerable part of the demands made by Mr. Couturier in his exposé, namely those concerning the independence and freedom of the liberal professions. This was particularly underlined by the remarks made by Mr. Möckershoff, President of the German Bundessteuerberaterkammer, and the general concern for the matter expressed here. For this reason I ask that an addition be made on page 3, in paragraph a, the wording of which I suggest be as follows: "... which would guarantee both the freedom of exercise of the profession and keep those who are not members of the profession from influencing it".

Then I have another suggestion, regarding the whole layout of the resolution. It deals with two main questions, first of all on the practice of our profession, on which we certainly must take a stand and the other point is on the harmonization of taxes. We should also voice our opinions on this, who else but us is called to do so? However, I wonder if it is a good idea to include both points in a single resolution, one runs the risk of reading at the beginning what has been said on taxes, and our statement on the profession may then seem to be too short. One should perhaps divide the resolution into two distinct parts.

Mr. Paul Puyraveau, Président of the "Institut Francais des Conseils Fiscaux (France)

Especially, after all M. le Directeur des Impôts who represents our Ministry for Finance, has said very rightly, I will appear in a very utopian light. But I feel that the true function of a Congress is to anticipate. However, in the resolution draft which I approve of fully, there is a point which I feel is important and which has not been touched on. I know that in so doing, I will somewhat leave our field. But has it not been said that we are above all economic counsels? And economics is taxation. Indeed we are in a position to know so. But economics is also more and more social politics. And when one speaks of taxes on income and in a general way of all taxes on the Gross National Product can we suggest that there is a true harmonization even if one succeeded in harmonizing taxes by means of income taxes, if there still are the distortions we have at present regarding social welfare contributions. I feel it is impossible to disconnect both these elements of national or regional taxes on the gross national income even if the first of these two may seem to be a redistribution of income. This is true in theory but it is much less true in the practice of economy.

Dr. Wilfried Dann, Steuerberater (Germany)

I would like to take up Mr. Wachter's proposition. I would like to suggest that the two previous paragraphs be shortened. We could say: "It is possible to envisage in theory the introduction of a net wealth tax. However, the considerable disadvantages as well as reasons of economic policy and the practical experience made to date do not speak in its favour."

Mr. Uberto Amorosi (Italy)

Just two short words to draw the attention of the Assembly on two points. In the second paragraph where it says: "differences still existing at present in national tax legislations ..." would it not be a good idea to add "... and in their application regulations"? We should not forget that there are countries where the application of the law constitutes a hindrance to free competition. We have rules which do not concern taxation, which are, for example, the rules on national accounting and which hinder certain compensations as between taxes already paid and taxes which still have to be paid. And in certain cases this is very expensive. They form a very real hindrance to the free setting up of subsidiary companies and to the freedom of business. Some laws do not state specifically the responsability of civil servants. Some laws allow long delays for the revision of the tax base. There are also those countries which grant tax information, that is to say that the tax payer can, before contracting, ask the advice of the authorities and then decide. That too is very important for the freedom of competition. So I would suggest that one add at that point "... and their application regulations ...", consequently, I would advise that one add at the end of the resolution a phrase such as: "So as to attain the objectives which this Congress considers important the Confederation will build Committees which are to work out detailed material on the various systems so as to be of assistance to the national member organizations and to the appropriate administrations.

My second remark is a thought which is perhaps a little freudian. It is stated at the beginning. "Profit determination and professional incomes should be sought according to accounting results." I would put this at the end because we are the ones concerned by professional incomes, and I would always put myself last.

Mr. Pierre Gastineau, conseil fiscal (France)

I would like to say a few words of the fifth paragraph of the draft resolution which in the English version reads: "Profit determination should be sought according to accounting results". This is taking it from the accounting definition of profits. I doubt whether this is not a false solution and a lazy solution. Why? Because there is no exact accounting definition of profit. About one year ago a certain number among us, were present at the meeting of the International Fiscal Association in Vienna, where we had discussed in particular the treatment of inflation. We had to admit in fact that there is no technical solution to the problem of inflation. A few miles away from here, on the other side of the Rhine where inflation only amounts to about 2 or 3 % it is considered negligeable. In France, when we multiply by 3, 4 or 5 the same rate, we feel that it is a phenomenon which is of some importance. If we go to the other side of the Alpes or on the other side of the Channel it then becomes a considerable phenomenon. And we have to admit that accounting techniques have not yet been able to find a solution. Consequently, to try to base oneself on apparent technical data, accounting data which has all the appearance of being exact to the nearest penny or centime, is something quite inexact. And although this is so I have no alternative solution ready. We are faced with a problem which has caused vast difficulties and I think it would be quite dangerous to set as principle that we refer purely and simply to accounting data.

Prof. Dr. Horst Vogel, Steuerberater and Rechtsanwalt (Germany)

I think we have made a considerable step forward by mentioning the 4th directive. The preceding speaker has, it seems, - pardon me - not yet read the 4th directive. We have a uniform directive on evaluation and showing in balance sheet form for all companies, public companies and limited liability companies and in that respect a basis for harmonization and for profit determination for tax purposes. I ask that this last statement requesting that this part be once more crossed off, not be accepted.

Prof. Dr. Albert Tiberghien, President of the C.F.E. (Belgium)

I would now like to give Prof. Couturier the floor. I suggest that we do not adopt a resolution but that we discuss a text on the cooperation of tax consultants in companies. Mr. Couturier has written a text which we could use vis-à-vis the EEC authorities and which we could send to the press, at any rate, which will be printed in the book which you will be sent and which includes all the papers and discussions which have taken place.

Prof. Dr. Jos. J. Couturier, conseil fiscal (Belgium)

I would first of all like to apologize. For the reason known to you now, I unfortunately was not able to hold personally the exposé which you asked me to prepare for this, our First European Congress. May I thank the President for having taken over that task and may I avail of this opportunity also, to thank warmly all the different colleagues in all the countries of the Community, who were kind enough to send me some documentation for this paper.

Time is now pressing on and I would like to read to you a résumé of the paper in the form of a draft resolution:

The Congress, having noted that the work of the tax consultant consists of three different essential functions, namely: preventive counsel, the carrying out of writings such as declarations and other acts and the representation of the tax payer in front of administrative authorities and of the judiciary; noting that the profession of the tax consultant needs to be organized legally in all the countries of the Community, noting that the tax consultant works in fields where other liberal professions are also active, namely solicitors, notaries, chartered accountants, that the work of these different professions is often complementary and that cooperation should exist not only between members of the same discipline, but also among members of many of these disciplines, if not, of all these disciplines, within appropriate professional associations and this not only on the national level but also on the international level; noting all this, the Congress adopts the following recommendations:

1. As regards the profession of the tax consultant, in countries where it has not yet been done, the organization of the profession of tax consultant must be pursued by every means possible, taking the triple function of the profession into account: counsel, assistance with writings, assistance in the case of law suits. So as to promote interprofessional cooperation the disciplinary procedures to which the tax consultant is subjected must be comparable to that of other liberal professions with which he is likely to cooperate.
2. Regarding professional cooperation, the tax consultant must

be able to practice his profession either individually, or in groups, or within associations, or within appropriate civil or commercial companies, or as a collaborator of another tax consultant or group of tax consultants.

3. Regarding interprofessional cooperation, with view of the pressures of social evolution, lasting professional associations among representatives of different liberal professions should be encouraged and made legally possible in the field of tax consulting. It is important, not that the professions in question be regulated by virtue of the law, rather it is important that they be governed by disciplinary regulations which are sufficiently equivalent, to enable the existence of a lasting interprofessional association in each of the countries of the European Communities. Each of the participating professions must be assured independence in interprofessional associations.

4. Regarding international interprofessional cooperation all hindrances caused either by provisions of law or regulations which hinder the freedom of association either among persons belonging to the same profession or among persons belonging to different liberal professions should be eliminated either by the legislative road which created them and/or the regulations. The example given by the Parisian and British has shown that Community Directives however desirable they might have been are not indispensable to the setting up of cooperation agreements, even beyond frontiers.

Prof. Dr. Albert Tiberghien, President of the C.F.E. (Belgium)

First of all regarding Prof. Couturier's text, do you wish to adopt it? ...

Mr. Couturier's remark are most interesting. They contain certainly many things which most of us would agree with. But there are a series of points which would need to be discussed. I think that the rest of the time we have available this morning will not suffice to discuss a number of different points, so e. g. the description of the activities. We would certainly have here a number of remarks to make. I think Mr. Couturier's work will serve as an excellent basis for our work, and a discussion should be held on this basis at a later date so as to - because it is too detailed and profound - arrive at a statement which we could all adhere to. It would certainly be good of an appropriate committee of the Confédération Fiscale Européenne were to examine the suggestion made by Mr. Couturier. They are really most useful but on the grounds of a number of certainly different opinions it is not possible to adopt it yet.

Prof. Dr. Albert Tiberghien, President of the C.F.E. (Belgium)

Fine, I was a bit too hasty. The next meeting of our Confédération Fiscale Européenne will take place in two months in Frankfurt. I suggest that we discuss the text proposed by Mr. Couturier which will certainly serve as an interesting starting point and which, I am sure, will not be changed much. As regards the resolution proper of this Congress, I ask you to give us full warrant to act for the best so that we write something coherent, taking the remarks made regarding taxes on capital, in particular, into account.

Resolution

PREMIER CONGRES EUROPEEN DES CONSEILS FISCAUX

ERSTER EUROPA-KONGRESS DER STEUERBERATER

FIRST EUROPEAN TAX CONSULTANTS' CONGRESS

13th and 14th October 1978

Final Resolution

For the first time tax consultants from all the European countries have convened in congress. For their meeting, attended by political representatives and by high level civil servants from the Institutions of the European Community and from each of the member states, they have chosen Strasbourg, the city of Europe. Under the heading "Fiscalité en Europe" the papers read and the debates served the purpose of stock-taking and of working for the goal of tax and professional law harmonization in Europe.

Differences still existing at present in national tax legislations and in their application regulations as well as in the various other duties lead to distortions in competition among companies within the European Communities. They are contrary to the fundamental goal which the member states had set themselves when they signed the Treaty of Rome, i.e. that of futhering a harmonious development of economic life.

Although considerable progress has been made with regard to the harmonization of customs duties and of the basis on which Value-Added-Tax is determined, the harmonization of tax on income and on profits remains insufficient.

Tax consultants from the European Communities countries convened for their First European Congress organized by the Confédération Fiscale Européenne (C.F.E.) believe that efforts should be made in the following fields in particular :

I. Tax law

a) Profit determination should be sought according to accounting results. A common solution to the problem of the relationship between commercial and tax accounting on the basis of the 4th E.E.C. directive (Directive on the drawing up of balance sheets) would be an important contribution to harmonization in the field of profit determination. This calls for a unification of regulations regarding e.g. valuations, provisions, depreciation systems, as well as fiscal and non fiscal subsidies. Regulations concerning tax exemptions and tax rates should be gradually harmonized.

b) Double taxation of company profits both at the companies' level and in addition at the shareholders' level, be it full or partial, should be avoided. A uniformed imputation system by means of tax credit should be introduced for all income taxes collected in the name of one of the European Community States.

c) It is possible to envisage in theory the introduction of a net wealth tax. However its considerable disadvantages as well as reasons of economic policy and the practical experience made to-date do not speak in its favour.

Professional law

The tax consultant's profession is an international one. Its field of activity should not be restricted by national frontiers. Clients from all the economic and professional sectors represent the wide span of the European economy. Tax consultants consider the following points indispensable to the futher development of their professional activities:

a) Their professional rights and duties must be shaped according to uniform principles within the European countries, which would guarantee both the freedom of exercise of the profession and keep those who are not members of the profession from influencing it;

b) after the harmonization of the law of the profession measures will have to be taken to facilitate the rendering of services by tax consultants across frontiers;

c) co-operation among tax consultants and with other related liberal professions must be encouraged, and obstacles contrary to this remouved;

d) permanent international institutions must be established and developped by the professional organizations so as to permit a continuous exchange of views.

Closing Address of the President of the C.F.E.

Translated from French by Roselle Prill du Pradal

Ladies and Gentlemen, dear colleagues,

We have now arrived at the end of the Congress, and the moment has come to express thanks, to congratulate and perhaps also to criticize. May I first of all extend may thanks and my congratulations to our interpreters, who had the difficult task of understanding our technical language of tax specialists. Our team splendidly mastered the difficult task of interpreting at a tax congress.

We owe a special word of thanks to our Secretary General, Mr. Gerhard, who has organized and prepared this Congress and proved to us once more his talent for organization and his sense of efficiency.

May I also thank our Vice-President, Dr. Dann, for his most useful collaboration in the organization of the Congress and in particular the Bundessteuerberaterkammer, represented by its President, Mr. Möckershoff, without whose help we would not have been able to master the enormous amount of administrative work tied to the preparation of such a Congress.

Now for the criticism: The invitations to the congress were unfortunately sent out too late in some countries. Members of the profession and guests should receive the invitations at least three months before the beginning of the Congress.

Furthermore it would be useful if the speakers could send their papers in good time to the Congress Secretariat so that they could be printed and handed out at the Congress. As a result, the participants could read the papers before the Congress, their oral presentation would take less time and the discussions could be longer, so that a larger number of participants at the Congress could take part in the so important discussions.

The First European Tax Consultants' Congress ever to have taken place is a success. It was certainly necessary and useful for our profession to voice our opinions and our problems in Europe, and to do so in a European City.

With the help of the experience gained at the First Congress of European Tax Consultants, the C.F.E. will hold a Second Congress and will accept Dr. Lecce's invitation to go to Italy. We would like to choose Rome as City for the Congress, the City in which the Treaties laying down the foundation of the European Communities were signed.

I declare the Congress closed, thanking all the participants, and with the hope of seeing them again at the Second Congress of European Tax Consultants.

Attendance list

AIREY, Desmond, Chartered Accountant,
GB - London

ALTHERR, Günther, Steuerberater,
D - Bad Dürkheim

AMOROSI, Uberto, RAG./R.U.C.,
I - Mailand

ARENS, Wilfrid, Finanzpräsident,
D - Saarbrücken

ARM, Wolfgang, Steuerberater,
D - Quierschied

ARNOLD, Anthony, Taxation Adviser,
GB - London

AUDEKERKE, Paule van, Expert comtable/Conseil Fiscal,
B - Oostende

BACHMANN, Heinz, Dipl.-Kfm., Geschäftsführer des Deutschen Steuerberaterverbandes e.V.,
D - Bonn

BALE, Norman, Président de l'Institute of Taxation in Ireland
IR - Dublin

BALLIGAND, Henri, Conseil Fiscal,
B - Marcinelle

BANSE, Heribert, Student,
D - Worms

BARBIER, Etienne, Conseil Juridique et Fiscal,
F - Neuilly

BARDET, Henri, Conseil Juridique et Fiscal,
F - Neuilly

BARREA, Joseph, Conseil Fiscal,
B - Arlon

BARTSCH, Heinz, Steuerberater,
D - Köln

BATHY, Guy, Conseil Fiscal,
B - Lavacherie

BAUDIENVILLE, Guy, Conseil Juridique et Fiscal,
F - Lille

BAUMSTARK, Bernd, Steuerberater,
D - Rastatt

BECH, Melitta, Steuerbevollmächtigte,
D - Berlin

BECKER, Jürgen A., Wirtschaftsprüfer, Rechtsanwalt,
D - Saarbrücken

BECKER, Kurt, Dipl.-Kfm., Steuerberater,
D - Ludwigshafen

BECKMANN, Claus, Steuerbevollmächtigter,
D - Seesen

BECX, Arnold, Federatie Belastingconsulent,
NL - Knegsel

BEHRENS, Carl, Dipl.-Kfm.,
D - Alfeld

BELL, Manfred, Steuerbevollmächtigter,
D - Gerolstein

BERENDS, Nella, Steuerberaterin,
D - Emden

BERGER, Hans Victor, Steuerberater, Vizepräsident der Steuerberaterkammer Düsseldorf,
D - Krefeld

BERTORELLO, Dr. Stefano,
I - Milano

BERTRANO, Jacques, Conseil Juridique et Fiscal,
F - Paris

BETTE, Augusto, Administrateur Principal, Rat der Europäischen Gemeinschaften,
B - Brüssel

BETTINCK, Jan W., Belastingadviseur,
NL - Huizen

BEUL, Herbert, Steuerberater,
D - Neuwied

BEYLER, Robert, Directeur Général du Palais de la Musique et des Congres, F - Straßburg

BIANCHI, Dr. Silvio, Steuerberater,
CH - Basel

BIHR, Dr. Dietrich, Steuerberater, Wirtschaftsprüfer,
D - Karlsruhe

BLUMENSTEIN, Gerold, Ministerialdirigent im Niedersächsischen Ministerium der Finanzen,
D - Hannover

BÖTTCHER, Dr. Hans-Georg, Direktor der Bundessteuerberaterkammer,
D - Bonn

BOEYE, Anton, Reviseur d'entreprise,
B - Anvers

BOHN, Rainer, Steuerbevollmächtigter,
D - Bad Kreuznach

BOINET, Bernard, Conseil Juridique et Fiscal,
F - Laon

BOKKES, Jan, Feteratie Belastingconsulent,
NL - Arnhem

BOLLEN, Guy, Conseiller Juridique,
B - Brüssel

BOMBARDELLA, F. Pasetti, Directeur Général du Cabinet du Président du Parlament Européen,
L - Luxemburg

BORNHEIM, Paul, Steuerberater, Wirtschaftsprüfer, Präsident des Bundesverbandes der Steuerberater e.V.,
D - Eitorf

BOUCHARD, Jean, Conseil Juridique et Fiscal,
F - Neuilly

BOURSOT, Jean-François, Conseil Juridique et Fiscal,
F - Straßburg

BRENNER, Eberhard, Steuerberater,
D - Bruchsal

BREUER, Christiane, Dipl.-Kfm., Steuerberaterin,
D - München

BROUWERS, Bart, Conseiller Fiscal,
NL - 's-Hertogenbosch

BRUIGOM, den Pieter, Belastingadviseur,
NL - Apeldoorn

BRUNO, Claude, Juridique Fiscal, Directeur Général,
F - Paris

BUCK, Carl, Steuerberater,
D - Hamburg

BUCKEL, Albert, Dipl.-Kfm., Steuerberater, Ehren-Vizepräsident der C.F.E.,
D - München

BÜHNEMANN, Hans, Geschäftsführer,
D - Schöningen

BÜRK, Gilbert, Steuerbevollmächtigter,
D - Bruchsal

BURCHARDT, Prof. Dr. Paul, Steuerberater, Rechtsanwalt,
D - Berlin

BURGGRAAF, John,
NL - Dordrecht

BURKE, Richard, Mitglied der Kommission der Europäischen Gemeinschaften,
B - Brüssel

CAPPELLE, Luc, Conseiller Fiscal,
B - Deurle

CARBIENER, Bernard, Dolmetscher,
F - Straßburg

CAZENAVE, Raymond, Conseil Juridique et Fiscal,
F - Amiens

CHASSAGNY, A., Conseil Juridique et Fiscal,
F - St. Marcel

CHAUVIÈRE, Michel, Journalist, Rédacteur en Chef adjoint du "Nouvel Economiste",
F - Paris

CHEYNEL, Pierre, Conseil Juridique et Fiscal,
F - Levallois

CHIFFAUT-MOLIARD, Pierre, Conseil Juridique,
F - Paris

CODELLI, Ottavio, Avocat,
I - Triest

COHU, Robert, Conseil Juridique et Fiscal,
F - Paris

COLAJANNI, Dott. Mosé-Pietro,
I - Mailand

COLLORIDI, Enrico, Commercialista,
I - Mailand

COMBASTET, Dr. Paul, Conseil Juridique et Fiscal,
F - Paris

COOLS, Albert, Secrétaire du Président de la C.F.E.,
B - Brüssel

COTTON, Jean, Vice-Président de l'Institut français des conseils Fiscaux,
F - Paris

CROXATTO, Prof. Gian Carlo, Mitglied des Steuerausschusses der C.F.E.,
I - Genua

COULON, Jean-Claude, Conseil Juridique, Secrétaire Général de l'A.N.C.J.,
F - Paris

COUTURIER, Prof. Dr. Jos. J., Conseil Fiscal,
B - Wilrijk

CRAYENCOUR, de Jean-Pierre, Secrétaire Général du S.E.P.L.I.S.,
B - Tervueren

DAHMEN, Eva Maria, Steuerbevollmächtigte,
D - Gusterath

DAHMEN, Josef, Steuerbevollmächtigte,
D - Gusterath

DAHMEN, Ursula, Studentin,
D - Gusterath

DAITZ, Wolf, Steuerberater,
D - Timmendorfer Strand

DANN, Dr. Dipl.-Kfm. Wilfried, Steuerberater, Präsident der Steuerberaterkammer Saarland, Vizepräsident der C.F.E.,
D - Saarbrücken

DEFOIN, Jean-M., Expert-Comptable, Conseiller Fiscal,
B - Namur

DEGROUX, Michel, Conseil Juridique,
F - Paris

DEKKER, Nicolas, Belastingadviseur,
NL - Bilthoven

DELTOUR, Robert, Conseil Fiscal,
F - Roubaix

DENIS, René, Expert Fiscal,
B - Viville

DÊPREZ, John, Conseil Fiscal
F - Paris

DEROECK, Raoul, Conseiller Fiscal,
B - Jumet

DEVERS, Maurice, Accountant NCAB,
B - Gent

DILLEN, Prof. Joris, Prof. Ficale Hogeschool,
B - Brüssel

DOELEMEYER, Dr. Hans-Joachim, Steuerberater,
D - Bad Homburg

DÖPKE, Willi, Steuerberater,
D - Bad Nenndorf

DOMBURG, Dr. van Jan,
NL - Dordrecht

DOYLE, Robert, Représentation Permanente d'Irlande auprès des Communautés Européennes, First Secretary,
B - Brüssel

DRINKENBURG, Frans, Directeur,
NL - 's-Gravenhage

DUTZ, Heinz E.A., Steuerberater,
D - Kiel

DUWEL, Robert, Directeur Général,
B - Gent

EBRARD, Henri, Conseil Juridique et Fiscal,
F - Neuilly

EGBERTS, Eckard, Steuerberater, Präsident der Steuerberaterkammer Niedersachsen,
D - Emden

EGER, Othmar, Steuerberater,
D - Oberndorf

EGGESIECKER, Dr. Fritz, Dipl.-Kfm., Dipl.-Volkw., Steuerberater,
D - Köln

EITSCHBERGER, Gustl, Geschäftsführerin der Steuerberaterkammer Stuttgart,
D - Stuttgart

ESSER, Christian, Steuerberater,
D - Siegburg

ESSER, Margret, Steuerbevollmächtigte,
D - Siegburg

FAIVRE, Michel, Conseil Juridique et Fiscal,
F - Levallois

FAUROUX, René, Conseil Juridique et Fiscal,
F - Neuilly

FAVIER, Jacques-Henri, Représentant de l'UEC,
F - Paris

FEUERHERDT, Friedhelm, Steuerberater,
D - Gummersbach

FEUGAS, Alain, Conseil Juridique et Fiscal,
F - Mantes la Jolie

FISCHER, Dr. Harry, Geschäftsführer beim Deutschen Industrie- und Handelstag,
D - Bonn

FLEURET, Dr. Jean,
F - Neuilly

FOSSEPREZ, Hubert, Directeur,
B - Leuven

FRANDSEN, IB, Attaché Fiscal, Représentation Permanente du Danemark,
B - Brüssel

FRANK, Erich, Dipl.-Volksw., Steuerberater,
D - Weiden

FRANKE, Horst Günter, Steuerberater,
D - Kiel

FRANKE, Kurt, Steuerberater,
D - Eislingen

FRANQUET, Raoul, Advisûer Fiscale,
B - Deurne

FREDERSDORF, Hermann, Mitglieder des Wirtschafts- und Sozialausschusses der Europäischen Gemeinschaften, Präsident der Europäischen Union der Steuerbeamten, Vorsitzender der Deutschen Steuer-Gewerkschaft, Stellvertr. Bundesvorsitzender des Deutschen Beamtenbundes,
D - Düsseldorf

FRENZEL, Jürgen, Dipl-Volksw., Steuerberater,
D - Karlsruhe

FREY, Herbert, Steuerbevollmächtigter,
D - Überlingen

FRICKE, Robert Erich, Oberregierungsrat im Bundesministerium für Wirtschaft,
D - Bonn

FRICKER, Bernard, Conseil Fiscal,
F - Illzach-Modenheim

FRISCH, Dr. Alfons, Dipl.-Kfm., Steuerberater, Wirtschaftsprüfer,
D - Saarbrücken

FOELICHER, M., Directeur du Banque Nationale de Paris,
F - Straßburg

FRY, Oliver G., Solicitor,
IR - Dublin

GAMBIER, Claude, Conseil Fiscal,
F - Neuilly

GARNIER, Alain, Conseil Juridique et Fiscal,
F - Neuilly

GASTINEAU, Pierre, Conseil Fiscal,
F - Levallois

GEMMEL, Heinz Dieter, Dipl.-Kfm., Steuerberater,
D - Saarbrücken

GÊRARD, Marcel, Trêsorier Principal des Finances de la Ville et de la Communautê urbaine de Strasbourg,
F - Straßburg

GERHARD, Karl-Heinz, Dipl.-Volksw., Generalsekretär der C.F.E., Hauptgeschäftsführer der Bundessteuerberaterkammer,
D - Bonn

GERHARD, Manuela,
D - Opladen-Lützenkirchen

GEUPEL, Willi, Steuerbevollmächtigter,
D - Oberweissenbach

GILARDI, Jean, Directeur de Societês,
F - Paris

GJUND, Kathy, Hostess,
F - Straßburg

GLAUTIER, Gisele, Conseillêre en Fiscalitê, Expert Comptable,
B - Namur

GÖBERT-LE PROVOST, Marga, Steuerberaterin,
D - Finnentrop

GOELLER, Else, Steuerberaterin,
D - Stuttgart

GOUSSET, Jean, Conseil Juridique et Fiscal,
F - Calais

GRAFE, Ernst-Dieter, Dipl.-Volksw., Steuerberater,
D - Troisdorf

GRASSI, Eduardo
I - Rom

GRIMLER, André, Conseil Fiscal,
F - Hirsinque

GRIMM, Horst, Dipl.-Volksw., Steuerberater,
D - Darmstadt

GÜRTZGEN, Dr. Winfried,
D - Düsseldorf

HAAG, Michel, Conseiller Fiscal,
B - Bastogne

HAERTEL, Gottfried, Steuerberater,
D - Kusel

HAGÈGE, Pierre, Conseil Juridique et Fiscal,
F - Le Chesmay

HANSEN, Dr. Jürgen, Dipl.-Volksw., Steuerberater,
D - Bad Segeberg

HART, t' Mr. Dr. Willem, Belastingadviseur,
NL - Apeldoorn

HECK, Walter, Steuerberater,
D - Leverkusen

HEIN, Albert, Steuerberater,
D - Saarburg

HEINING, Dr. Arnold, Rechtsanwalt, Generalsekretär der Deutschen Vereinigung für Internationales Steuerrecht, de la Chambre de Commerce Internationale,
D - Köln

HEINRICH, Hans, Dipl.-Volksw., Steuerberater,
D - Schwäbisch Gmünd

HENRIKSEN, Ole, Bus, Directeur Général, Commission of the European Communities,
B - Brüssel

HEISEL, Raymond, Directeur Régional des Impôts,
F - Straßburg

HENRY, André, Expert Comptable,
B - Brugge

HERFST, Hugo, Belastingadviseur,
NL - Arnhem

HERINGA, Dr. J.C. Joost, Tax Consultant,
NL - Aw Hoofddorp

HERMANT, Suzanne, Chef de Service Fiscal - Bouygues,
F - Paris

HEROLD, Dr. Hans, Steuerberater,
D - Montabaur

HERTLEIN, Herbert, Dipl.-Kfm., Steuerberater,
D - München

HERTZOG, Robert, Professeur de Droit Fiscal à la Fasulté de Droit de Strasbourg,
F - Straßburg

HILDENBRAND, Emil, Steuerberater,
D - Offenburg

HILLEN, Hans-Otto, Steuerberater,
D - Bremen

HILLMANN, Dr. Henning, Regierungsdirektor im Bundesministerium für Wirtschaft,
D - Bonn

HINZEMANN, Helga, Dipl.-Kfm., Steuerberaterin,
D - Köln

HOCHLENERT, Dieter, Steuerberater,
D - Neuwied

HOEBERIGS, Johannes, Federatie-Belastingconsulent,
NL - Roermond

HOEFELD, Dr. Ludwig, Steuerberater und Wirtschaftsprüfer,
D - Freiburg

HÖPFNER-WETZEL, Dr. Erna, Ministerialrätin beim Deutschen Bundestag,
D - Bonn

HÖRSTMANN, Dr. Franz, Dipl.-Kfm., Steuerberater, Vorsitzender des Fachinstituts der Steuerberater Köln e.V.,
D - Köln

HOFFMANN, Beatrice, Hostess,
F - Straßburg

HOFMANN, Alfred, Steuerberater,
D - Kassel

HOFSTRA, Prof. Dr. Hendrik Jan, Emeritierter Ordinarius für Steuerrecht an der Universität Leiden, ehem. Finanzminister der Niederlanden,
NL - Den Haag

HOPPE, Wilfried F.W., Steuerberater,
D - Hamburg

HORSTMANN, Ursula, Steuerberaterin,
D - Hille

HUG, Bernard, Directeur de la FIDUCIAIRE REGIONALE, Président de l'A.N.C.J.,
F - Straßburg

HUSS, Ursula, Steuerberaterin,
D - Köln

HUSS, Werner, Rechtsanwalt, Geschäftsführer in der Bundessteuerberaterkammer,
D - Köln

INGEN, van Pieter, Tax Consulent,
NL - Veenendaal

INSLEGERS, Robert, Expert Comptable,
B - Brugge

ISAACS, Sam S.A., Tax Consultant,
NL - Driebergen Rijsenburg

JACOB, Friedrich L., Steuerberater, Präsident der Steuerberaterkammer Rheinland-Pfalz,
D - Ludwigshafen

JOHNSTON, Robert, B.A. LLB.,
IR - Dublin

JONGBLOED, Ab, Maître of droit,
NL - Amsterdam

JONKER, E.J., Maître en droit,
NL - Amsterdam

JUNG, Robert, Dipl.-Kfm., Steuerberater, Vizepräsident des Deutschen Steuerberaterverbandes e.V.,
D - Pirmasens

KAHN-ACKERMANN, Georg, Serêtaire Gênéral du Conseil de l'Europe,
F - Straßburg

KALLMEIER, Elke, Sekretärin,
D - Hannover

KANDEL, Günter, Steuerberater,
D - Seesen

KARMANN, Dieter, Geschäftsführer,
D - Königsbrunn

KARMANN, Ruth, Steuerberaterin,
D - Königsbrunn

KASPER, Hans Gerd, Steuerberater,
D - St. Georgen

KAWALLE, Maria, Dipl.-Kfm., Dolmetscherin,
D - Köln

KEMPELMANN-NOBER, Lore, Steuerberaterin,
D - Essen

KERGALL, Yann, Conseil Juridique et Fiscal,
F - Neuilly

KERN, Dieter F., Steuerberater,
D - Stuttgart

KEUSSEN, Dieter, Steuerberater,
D - Krefeld

KEYMOLEN, Paul Charles, Expert Comtable,
B - Brüssel

KIECKSEE, Helmut, Steuerberater,
D - Rendsburg

KLEBES, Marie-Louise, Dolmetscherin,
F - Straßburg

KLIMESCH, Gerhard, Steuerberater,
D - Karlsruhe

KOCH, Gérard, Conseil Juridique,
F - Mulhouse

KOEVOETS, Harry A., Conseiller Fiscal,
B - Anvers

KOTTWITZ, Juergen, Steuerberater,
D - Oberursel

KOTTWITZ, Ruth, Bürovorsteherin,
D - Oberursel

KRAHFORST, Helmut, Steuerberater,
D - Eitorf

KRALLMANN, Karl, Steuerberater, Wirtschaftsprüfer, Rechtsanwalt,
D - Saarbrücken

KRAMMIG, Karl, Steuerberater,
D - Bonn

KREPPEL, Dr. Thomas, Fachanwalt für Steuerrecht,
D - München

KROOS, Hans, Dipl.-Kfm., Steuerberater, Wirtschaftsprüfer,
D - Hannover

KRUSE, Dr. Hans-Gerhard, Steuerberater, Wirtschaftsprüfer,
D - Marburg

KÜNDGEN, Peter, Steuerberater,
D - Bad Neuenahr

KNÜFFNER, Dr. Peter, Steuerberater, Wirtschaftsprüfer,
D - Landshut

KÜHN, Hans, Steuerberater,
D - Pirmasens

KUGLER, Robert, Directeur du Bureau de la Société Juridique et Fiscale,
F - Straßburg

KUNEN, K.C., Taxadvisor,
NL - Rotterdam

KUNERT, Berhard, Steuerberater,
D - Köln

KUNKEL, Peter, Steuerbevollmächtigter,
D - Lübeck

KUNST, Gesine, Steuerbevollmächtigte,
D - Wiesbaden

KUNST, Peter, Steuerbevollmächtigter,
D - Wiesbaden

KUPFER, Gerhard, Dipl.-Kfm., Steuerberater,
D - Kehl

KURZ, Karin, Steuerbevollmächtigte,
D - Essen

KUTTER, Heinz, Präsident des Finanzgerichts München,
D - München

LABSCH, Dr. Nobert Horst, Dipl.-Volksw., Steuerberater,
D - Achern

LA FONTA, Edouard, Conseil Fiscal,
F - Neuilly

LAMBRECHTS, François, Conseil Fiscal,
B - Liege

LASCHET, Franz Florian, Rechtsanwalt, Deutsche Gruppe der Internationalen Handelskammer,
D - Köln

LASSAYS, Antoine, Conseil Juridique et Fiscal,
F - Mantes la Jolie

LECLAIR, Georges,
NL - Wilrijk

LECCE, Dr. Salvatore, Avocat-Docteur en Economie, Secrétaire Général de l'A.N.T.I.,
I - Mailand

LEERMAN, Albert, Expert comptable - Conseil Fiscal,
B - Oostende

LEONE, Dr. Lorenzo,
I - Mailand

LEONHARD, Martha, Steuerberaterin,
D - Mannheim

LEPERRE, Jean-Pierre, Conseil Juridique et Fiscal,
F - Marseille

LEPERRE, Rosette, Conseil Juridique et Fiscal,
F - Marseille

LESSU, Bernard, Conseil Juridique et Fiscal,
F - Bailhy

LIST, Prof. Dr. Heinrich, Präsident des Bundesfinanzhofes,
D - München

LIZAMBARD, Jean-Jacques, Conseil Juridique et Fiscal,
F - Neuilly

LOIR, Roger, Conseil Jurdique et Fiscal,
F - Lille

LONGIN, Franz, Steuerberater,
D - Stuttgart

LORENZ, Rainer, Steuerberater,
D - Hannover

LUCHT, Hildegard, Steuerberaterin,
D - Lübeck

LÜDICKE, Heinz, Steuerberater,
D - Duisburg

LUMPP, Dieter, Steuerbevollmächtigter,
D - Stuttgart

LUTZ, Albert, Steuerbevollmächtigter,
D - Achern

LUTZ, Kurt Fr., Steuerberater,
D - Kehl

MAES, Albert, Administrateur,
B - Oostende

MADRIGAL, Emmanuel, Licencié en droit - Conseil Juridique et Fiscal, Commissaire aux Comptes,
F - Paris

MANNES, Peter, Dipl.-Kfm., Steuerberater,
D - Lindlar

MARTIN, Heinz, Dipl.-Kfm., Steuerberater, Vizepräsident der Steuerberaterkammer Rheinland-Pfalz,
D - Kaiserslauten

MASSON, Olivior, Conseil Juridique et Fiscal,
F - Neuilly

MATHEN, Georges, Conseil Fiscal, Expert-Comptable,
B - Saint-Servais

MAUGUÉ, Jacques, Conseil Fiscal,
F - Paris

MAUS, Erich, Leitender Regierungsdirektor in der Oberfinanzdirektion Koblenz,
D - Koblenz

MAUTES, Manfred, Steuerberater,
D - Merzig

MAZEROLLES, Adrien, Trésorier Payeur Général de la Région d'Alsace,
F - Straßburg

MC LEAN, Donald, Past President of the Institute of Taxation,
IR - Greystones

MÉARY, Jean, Delegué Général de l'Association Nationale des Sociétés par Actions,
F - Paris

MEISTER, Dr. Norbert, Steuerberater, Rechtsanwalt,
D - Frankfurt

MENNEL, Dr. Annemarie, Ministerialrätin im Bundesministerium der Finanzen,
D - Bonn

MERTEN, Rudolf, Steuerberater,
D - Wiesbaden

MICHEL, Bernard, Conseil Juridique et Fiscal,
F - Castres

MIEHLER, Dr. Kurt, Ministerialrat im Bayerischen Staatsministerium der Finanzen,
D - München

MÖCKERSHOFF, Hubert, Steuerberater, Präsident der Bundessteuerberaterkammer,
D - Köln

MÖßMER, Erwin, Steuerberater, Wirtschaftsprüfer,
D - München

MOLL, Ernst, Dipl.-Kfm., Steuerberater,
D - Düren

MOULIN, Georges, Chef de la Division des Affaires Economiques du Conseil de l'Europe,
F - Straßburg

MOUTERDE, Jacques, Président de l'Union Professionnelle des sociétés Juridiques et fiscales,
F - Levallois

MÜLLER, Hans-Werner, Steuerbevollmächtigter,
D - Lollar

MÜLLER, Max-Carl, Steuerberater,
D - Staufen

MÜLLER, Lothar, Ministerialdirektor im Bayerischen Staatsministerium der Finanzen,
D - München

MUUSS, Harro, Ministerialrat im Bundesministerium der Finanzen,
D - Bonn

NÄTHKE, Dr. Karl, Dipl.-Kfm., Steuerberater,
D - Itzehoe

NIRO, Dr. Andrea,
I - Rom

NOEL, Louis, Conseil Juridique,
F - Saint-Marcel

NOEMIE, Michel, Conseil Juridique et Fiscal,
F - Levallois

NOLTE, Karl-Heinrich, Leitender Ministerialrat im Ministerium der Finanzen des Landes Nordrhein-Westfalen,
D - Düsseldorf

NORD, Hans R., Generalsekretär des Europäischen Parlaments,
L - Luxemburg

OESTERLE-MÖLLMANN, Heinz, Steuerbevollmächtigter,
D - VS-Schwenningen

OESTERLE-MÖLLMANN, Helene, Steuerbevollmächtigte,
D - VS-Schwenningen

OETTINGER, Hermann, Steuerberater, Wirtschaftsprüfer, Präsident der Steuerberaterkammer Stuttgart,
D - Ditzingen

OLIVIER, Bernard, Conseil Juridique et Fiscal,
F - La Madeleine

OLSEN, Henning Argyl, Registreret Revisor,
DK - Nykøbing Falster

OSTER, Hans, Steuerberater, Präsident der Steuerberaterkammer Schleswig-Holstein,
D - Kappeln

OTTERSBACH, Wolfgang, Steuerberater,
D - Siegburg

PACQUE, Pierre, Expert Fiscal,
B - Neuprez

PANIER, André, Conseil Fiscal,
B - Charleroi

PATTON, Susan, Dolmetscherin,
F - Straßburg

PEETERS, Frans, Conseiller Fiscal,
B - Antwerpen

PERREAU, Alain, Conseil Juridique et Fiscal,
F - Straßburg

PETER, Helmut, Ministerialdirektor im Finanzministerium des Saarlandes,
D - Saarbrücken

PETERSDORFF, v. Ingeborg, Assistentin des Generalsekretärs,
D - Bonn

PETIT, Guy, Luc, Conseil Fiscal,
F - La Rochelle

PFEIFFER, Dr. Gerd, Präsident des Bundesgerichtshofes,
D - Karlsruhe

PFLIMLIN, Pierre, Bürgermeister der Stadt Straßburg,
F - Straßburg

PICKERILL, Reginald, Taxation Adviser,
GB - Epping

PIETERS, Robert, Accountant, Belastingconsulent,
B - Gent

PINI, Wolfgang, Direktor im Generalsekretariat des Rates der Europäischen Gemeinschaften,
B - Brüssel

PIRARD, René, Conseil Fiscal,
B - Namur

POLLMEIER, Wilhelm, Steuerberater, Präsident der Steuerberaterkammer Westfalen-Lippe,
D - Bochum

POTHIER, Jean-Claude, Conseil Juridique,
F - Neuilly

PRILL DU PRADAL, Roselle, Dolmetscherin,
D - Bonn

PUTTEMANS, John, Conseil Fiscal,
D Machelen

PUYRAVEAU, Paul, Président de l'Institut Français des Conseils Fiscaux,
F - Paris

PYNE-GILBERT, Douglas, Chartered Accountant,
GB - London

QUISQUATER, Raymond, Accountant,
B - Brasschaat

QUITMANN, Dr. Werner, Steuerberater, Wirtschaftsprüfer,
D - Köln

RÄDLER, Dr. Albert, Steuerberater,
D - München

RADENNE, Roger, Conseil Fiscal,
F - Paris

RASCH, Hans-Joachim, Steuerberater,
D - Vechta

RASKOB, Helmut, Präsident des Finanzgerichts Rheinland-Pfalz,
D - Neustadt an der Weinstr.

REALE, Ulrico, Rechtsanwalt,
USA - Washington

REGER, Gerhard, Steuerberater, Wirtschaftsprüfer,
D - Frankfurt

REICHERT, Dieter, Steuerberater,
D - Wadern

REYNAUD, Charles, Secretaire Général du l'Union Professionnelle des Societes Juridiques et Fiscales,
F - Levallois

REYNAUD-CHAPPAZ, Maurice, Conseil Juridique et Fiscal,
F - Chambery

RICHTER, Jürgen, Dipl.-Volksw., Steuerberater,
D - Hamburg

RIJNBOUTT, Joost, Rax Consultant,
NL - Papendrecht

RISO, de Dr. Giovanno,
I - Mailand

ROBERT, Marcel, President du Cabinet "Fiscalite et Sociétes",
F - Besançon

RÖBEN, Dr. Johannes B.H., Direktor bei Kluver Law and Taxation Publishers,
NL - Deventer

ROELEN, Martin, Belastingconsulent,
NL - Arnhem

ROEST-CROLLIUS, MR. A.E., Belastingadviseur,
NL - Pijnacker

RONCA, Stefan, Rechtsanwalt,
CH - Basel

ROOSWINKEL, André, Belastingconsulent,
NL - Ede

RUBEL, Conrad M., Steuerberater,
D - Bergisch Gladbach

RUDOLPH, Martin, Ministerialdirektor im Bundesministerium der Justiz,
D - Bonn

SAINT-BAUZEL, Dr. Jacques, Conseil Juridique et Fiscal, Trésaurier de la C.F.E.,
F - Levallois

SAUMET, Pierre, Directeur Général, Conseil Juridique et Fiscal,
F - Levallois

SASS, Gert, EG-Abteilungsleiter, Kommission der Europäischen Gemeinschaften,
B - Brüssel

SCIBELLI, Dr. Carlo,
I - Venise

SEEBACH, Emil, Steuerberater,
D - Pirmasens

SEMPRINI, Uso, Directeur General des Impôts Indirectes,
I - Rom

SERCEAU, Roger, Conseil Juridique et Fiscal,
F - Bordeaux

SEYBOLD, Wolfgang, Leitender Ministerialrat in der Finanzbehörde der Stadt Hamburg,
D - Hamburg

SMID, Roelof, Taxlawyer,
NL - Rotterdam

SMITH, John W., Chartered Accountant,
GB - Richmond

SOMBSTAY, Jean-Pierre, Adjoint et Directeur Fiscal,
F - Paris

SONTAG, Helmuth F., Steuerbevollmächtigter,
D - Hildesheim

SPIELMANN, F. Kathy, Palais de la Musique et des Congrès,
F - Straßburg

SPOFFORTH, Michael Gordon, President of the Institute of Taxation,
GB - London

SÜDMEIER, Wilhelm, Steuerberater,
D - Minden

SURAMY, Maurice,
F - Paris

SUTHOFF, Horst, Steuerberater,
D - Braunschweig

SUTNER, Erich, Steuerberater,
D - Ingolstadt

SWART, Dr. Carl, Dipl.-Kfm., Chefredakteur "Der Betrieb",
D - Düsseldorf

SCHÄFER, Antonius, European Tax Advisor,
B - Brüssel

SCHÄFER, Hermann, Steuerberater,
D - Kehl

SCHAUBER, Dr. Wolfgang, MdB,
D - Bonn

SCHIL, van Karl, Accountant,
B - Antwerpen

SCHLECKER, Dr. Paul, Steuerberater, Vizepräsident der Steuerberaterkammer Südbaden,
D - Freiburg

SCHMIDT, Albert, Steuerberater,
D - Stuttgart

SCHMITT, Albert F., Conseiller Communautaire - Président de la Commission des Finances du Conseil de la Communauté Urbaine de Straßburg
F - Straßburg

SCHMITT-THOMAS, Lieselotte, Steuerberaterin,
D - Frankfurt

SCHMITT-THOMAS, Torsten-Olov,
D - Frankfurt

SCHOLLMAYER, Michael, Dipl.-Kfm., Steuerberater,
D - Mainz

SCHRÖDER, Horst, Dipl.-Kfm., Steuerberater,
D - Bingen

SCHÜTZ, H. Peter, Steuerberater,
D - Möglingen

SCHULTHEISS, Hannetraud, Steuerberaterin, Konsul von Malta,
D - Mainz

SCHULZ, Eckehard, Steuerberater,
D - Dannenberg

SCHULZ, Otto, Betriebswirt (Grad.), Steuerbevollmächtigter,
D - Berlin

SCHULTZE, Wolfgang, Steuerberater,
D - Achern

SCHWEIZER, Hans-Jürgen, Steuerbevollmächtigter,
D - Mannheim

SCHWER, Norbert, Dipl.-Volksw., Steuerberater,
D - Schonach

STADTAUS, Peter, Steuerbevollmächtigter,
D - München

STEINS, Anton, Steuerberater, Vizepräsident der Steuerberaterkammer Westfalen-Lippe,
D - Dortmund

STENDER, Hans, Steuerberater,
D - Kiel

STOFFEL, Ingo, Steuerberater,
D - Dorsten

STREICHENBERGER, Renaud, Conseil Juridique et Fiscal,
F - Neuilly

TAKX, Toon, Conseiller Fiscal,
B - Helmond

TE SPENKE, Gerrit, Tax Adviser,
NL - Amsterdam

TEUFEL, Prof. Eberhard, Steuerberater,
D - Tuttlingen

THERASSE, André, Conseiller Fiscal,
B - Brüssel

THOMAS, Dr. Christian, Assistent bei Kluwer Law and Taxation Publishers,
NL - Deventer

TIBERGHIEN, Prof. Dr. Albert, Conseil Fiscal, Präsident der C.F.E.,
B - Brüssel

TIMBART, Alban, Directeur du Service Fiscal du CONSEIL NATIONAL DU PATRONAT FRANCAIS, (C.N.P.F.),
F - Paris

TINAYRE, Alain, Avocat a la cour, Président de l'Union Nationale des Associations de Professions Libérales (UNAPL),
F - Paris

TOPP, Max-Egon, Dipl.-Kfm., Steuerberater,
D - Düsseldorf

TRISCHLER, Gilbert, Conseil Juridique et Fiscal,
F - Florange

TROUSSIER, Maurice, Conseil Juridique,
F - Levallois

TRUYEN, Lucienne, Belastingconsulente,
B - Gentbrugge

TURKO, Charles, Conseil Juridique et Fiscal,
F - Straßburg

ULRICH, Jochen, Steuerberater,
D - Kehl

UNTERBERG, Dr. Herbert, Ministerialrat im Ministerium für Wirtschaft, Mittelstand und Verkehr des Landes Nordrhein-Westfalen,
D - Düsseldorf

VAHL, Helmut F.G., Steuerberater,
D - Eisenberg

VALK, William, Dolmetscher,
F - Straßburg

VANADIA, Luigi,
I - Mailand

VANHORENBEECK, Walter, docteur en droit - conseil fiscal, Président de la Fédération Nationale des Fiduciaires, A.S.B.L. - Nationaal Verbond van Belastingconsulenten en Fiduciaires, V.Z.W.,
B - Gent

VANDEPERRE, Guy, Administrateur-Directeur,
B - Vilvoorde

VANNESTE, Frans A., Accountant, Fiscaal Adviseur,
B - Roeselare

VERTONGEN, Aloys, Administrateur-délégué S.A. FIDABEL,
B - Brüssel

VIESTER, Robert, Tax Consultant
NL - Nijmegen

VILLEGUERIN, de la François, Président de la Fiduciaire Juridique et Fiscale,
F - Paris

VIVIEN, Jean Philippe, Conseil Juridique et Fiscal,
F - Paris

VLEER, MR. Jacob,
NL - Rotterdam

VÖLZKE, Heinz, Oberamtsrat im Bundesministerium der Finanzen,
D - Bonn

VOGEL, Prof. Dr. Horst, Steuerberater, Rechtsanwalt, Geschäftsführendes Vorstandsmitglied des Instituts "Finanzen und Steuern",
D - Bonn

VOGEL, Joseph, Directeur de Préfecture,
F - Straßburg

VOGTS, Hans, Dipl.-Kfm., Steuerberater,
D - Köln

VOSKUHL, Joanna, Steuerberater,
D - Bad Herrenalb

WAARDENBURG, van Dirk A., Deputy Director, International Bureau of Fiscal Documentation,
NL - Amsterdam

WAASBERGEN, van Willem, Steuerberater, Wirtschaftsprüfer,
NL - Rotterdam

WACHTER, Winfried, Steuerberater, Präsident der Steuerberaterkammer München,
D - Memmingen

WALKER-SMITH, The Rt. Hon. Sir Derek, Q.C., M.P.,
GB - London

WARBRICK, Harry, Taxation Adviser,
GB - Shoal Hill, Cannock

WARDENIER, Hans, Fiscaal attaché, Représentation Permanente des Pays-Bas,
B - Brüssel

WARNING, Gerrit, Tax lawyer, Präsident de Nederlandse Orde van Belastingadviseurs,
NL - Amsterdam

WEBER, Klaus-Werner, Steuerbevollmächtigter,
D - Düsseldorf

WEBER-BLEYLE, M., Steuerberater, Rechtsanwält,
D - Reutlingen

WEHLER, Dr. Edmund, Steuerberater, Rechtsanwalt,
D - Frankfurt

WEHR, Herbert, Mairie de Strasbourg, Service des Relations Publiques,
F - Straßburg

WEGNER, Helmut, Steuerberater,
D - Bergen

WEILER, Dr. Heinrich, Dipl.-Volksw., Referent in der Bundessteuerberaterkammer,
D - Bonn

WENGER, Dr. Eduard, Dipl.-Kfm., Steuerberater,
D - Stuttgart

WERNER, Wolfram, Steuerberater, Wirtschaftsprüfer,
D - Völklingen

WESTBERG, Olaf, Dipl.-Kfm., Steuerberater,
D - Hamburg

WEYLAND, Anna-Leonie, Dipl.-Kfm., Steuerberaterin,
D - Worms

WEYLAND, Joseph, Représentation Permanente de Luxemburg,
B - Brüssel

WICHMANN, Jürgen, Steuerberater, Wirtschaftsprüfer,
D - Hannover

WIELINSKI, Nikolaus, Dipl.-Kfm., Steuerberater,
D - Esslingen

WIENEMANN, Dr. Eitel, Wirtschaftsprüfer,
D - Worms

WIERS, MR. Willem,
NL - Haarlem

WINGERDEN, van MR. Dick,
NL - Amsterdam

WINGERTER, Otto, Steuerberater,
D - Maikammer

WOELDERS, Dr. Hans, Tax Consultant,
NL - Leeuwarden

WOITKE, Peter W., Steuerberater,
D - Esslingen

WOLTER, Paul, Assessor, Hauptgeschäftsführer der Steuerberater-
kammer Düsseldorf,
D - Düsseldorf

WORSDALE-WASSMUTH, Gisela, Leiterin des Simultanteams,
F - Straßburg

WOSSILUS, Wolfgang, Steuerberater,
D - Berlin

WÜSTEN, Karl-Heinz, Steuerberater,
D - Köln

ZIEMENDORF, Brigitte, Steuerberaterin,
D - Berlin

ZIMMERMANN, Robert, Chef du Service de l'Organisation des Congrès,
F - Straßburg

ZUSCHKE, Dr. Ulrich, Kommission der Europäischen Gemeinschaften,
B - Brüssel

CONFÉDÉRATION FISCALE EUROPÉENNE
(C.F.E.)

La Pratique de la Fiscalité en Europe

SECOND EUROPEAN CONGRESS OF TAX CONSULTANTS

November 6th and 7th, 1980

ROME

GPSR Compliance

The European Union's (EU) General Product Safety Regulation (GPSR) is a set of rules that requires consumer products to be safe and our obligations to ensure this.

If you have any concerns about our products, you can contact us on ProductSafety@springernature.com

In case Publisher is established outside the EU, the EU authorized representative is:

Springer Nature Customer Service Center GmbH
Europaplatz 3
69115 Heidelberg, Germany

Batch number: 10845480

Printed by Printforce, the Netherlands